Get ready for an i[...] [...] move from the tyr[...] [...] family schedule that helps your whole family thrive! *Wise Moms* is a practical guide that shines light on every area of family life— marriage, communication, home, schedule, connection, and kids, with faith-centered advice, combined with the wisdom of real-life experience.

Mandy Arioto, CEO, The MomCo (MOPS International)

If you long for a friend who "gets you," who is vulnerable, practical, and wise in the ways of marriage and parenting, this author is your new friend. If you want to build a family upon a foundation of faith, this book is your guidebook. If you want a fun read with practical applications for your unique family, you will find them in this book! Grab three copies—one for you and two to give young moms!

Susan Alexander Yates, speaker; bestselling author of many books on parenting (SusanAlexanderYates.com)

In *Wise Moms*, Linda holds your hand and walks you through a beautiful process to discover the home you were created to build so it can become a reality and not just a dream. Rather than telling you what to do, she frees you to embrace and become the mother and home-builder God made you to be. This is the type of book that can produce quick wins as well as make a lasting impact for generations of your family. Read it, envision it, and have joy on the journey of building your dream home!

Cristin Parker, family advisor and coach; creator of "Your Family Blueprint"

Moms who are at any point in the learning curve will feel *seen*, *safe*, and *supported* under Linda's guidance. Like a master chef giving us access to her secret recipes, Linda offers up tested tips and tools to create a stronger, more satisfying family life. She empowers us as Chief Life Officers in our homes to better manage: our emotional responses, relational conflicts, decision-making, parenting issues, and how we engage with our own internal stories. She concludes each chapter with practical action items, resources, and reflection opportunities to personalize the takeaways and application steps. I highly recommend this resource.

Leslie L. Pitt, Licensed Marriage and Family Therapist

Wise Moms is a book of priceless value. If you come from a broken home, a home without Jesus at the center, or a Christian home that was lacking, then this book is for you. If you are a mom looking for wise advice on raising your kids, deepening your marriage, and nurturing your family, then this book is for you. If you are a new follower of Jesus and have no idea what it means to follow him in building a Christ-honoring home and family, then this book is for you.

Dr. Stacy Rinehart, founder, MentorLink International

I have known and watched Linda and Lloyd Reeb for many, many years as they've grown together in their relationship and as they've raised their family. They may be two of the most intentional people in terms of their spiritual growth that I know. Linda makes the statement that "no two moms are the same," which is an invitation to open this book and let it speak to you. So often Christian books are written based on formulas or mechanics. That is not the case with this book. Having raised five children of our own, my wife and I can say that it sure would've been nice to have this book when we got started. I recommended it wholeheartedly and with no reservation.

Ron Blue, author; founding director, Kingdom Advisors

With a blend of personal stories, biblical principles, and practical advice, Linda guides readers through the joys and challenges of marriage and parenting. Each chapter is filled with relatable stories and profound reflections, reminding readers of the importance of faith, love, and grace in building a healthy and strong marriage while parenting children. I loved that Linda doesn't make this journey a "one size fits all." Rather, she reminds the reader to rely on the Lord for daily guidance. I highly recommend this book to anyone who is embarking on the journey of motherhood!

Barb Foulkrod, mom and grandmother;
CEO, Hope Reins

Linda Reeb has dedicated years of work to strengthening marriages and families. Her experience and wisdom will add value to your life.

Linda Buford, philanthropist; wife of Bob Buford, who
founded The Halftime Institute

So practical! I absolutely loved the book and had to keep taking breaks to soak in Linda's knowledge and wisdom. I want so many friends to read it! The ideas and questions are radically biblical and insightful. If you want to learn how to prioritize God's best for your marriage and family, this is the book for you!

Marieke Desmond, mom, storyteller, and writer

I have invested decades of my life preparing faith-oriented college women for successful careers and lives. These talented women are also determined to become great mothers. Linda Reeb's book *Wise Moms* brings proven wisdom for women as they build thriving marriages and Christian families.

Nido Qubein, president, High Point University

Wise Moms deserves to hold a prominent place in every family's bookcase. Linda's book offers compelling insights on how to change from being on autopilot in our lives and with our families by guiding us in creating our own family vision based on our own personal values—not those our culture assumes for us. She takes us through the many phases of learning and adapting as families are formed and grow in their relationships with God and with each other. This inspiring book provides tangible actions we can take through the seasons of our family's spiritual growth toward healthy, happy families connected to God.

Don Wenner, bestselling author, *Building an Elite Organization*; founder and CEO, DLP Capital

LINDA RUTH REEB

WISE

MOMS

A GUIDE FOR BUILDING
YOUR HOME ON CHRIST

HIM
PUBLICATIONS

Nashville, Tennessee

himpublications.com

Wise Moms
Copyright © 2024 by Linda Ruth Reeb

Requests for information should be sent via email to HIM Publications. Visit himpublications.com for contact information.

Library of Congress Control Number: 2024934227

ISBN: 978-1-970102-90-1 (Paperback)
ISBN: 978-1-970102-95-6 (Hardcover)
ISBN: 978-1-970102-91-8 (ePub)

Editorial and art direction: Chad Harrington (himpublications.com)
Cover design and text design management: Bryana Anderle (himpublications.com)
Interior design: Marissa Meadows (youpublish.com)

To Lloyd. Without you this book would only be an idea.

To Mom, Ruth, and Leslie. Many thanks for
how you shaped and influenced me.

And to Beth Perryman, a world-class encourager.

CONTENTS

Acknowledgements   *11*

Introduction   *13*

Phase 1: The Foundation *Connection with God and Self*

1. Building Your House with God   *19*
2. Celebrating Mothers of Many Styles   *25*
3. Unpacking Your Life Story   *31*
4. Managing Your Emotions   *39*

Phase 2: The Walls and Roof *Connection with Spouse*

5. Building a Marriage-Centered Family   *47*
6. Keeping Your Love Alive   *55*
7. Learning Communication and Conflict Management   *61*
8. Considering Submission—A Bible Paradox   *69*

Phase 3: The Interior *Connection with Your Kids*

9. Nurturing Your Children's Spiritual Growth   *77*
10. Disciplining Your Children   *85*
11. Navigating Sexual-Wholeness Topics   *91*

Phase 4: The Windows and Doors *Connection with the World*

12. Creating a Family Vision Based on Your Values   *99*
13. Being a Chief Life Officer   *105*
14. Protecting Your Family from the Downside of Technology   *111*
15. Interacting as a Family of Faith in Today's World   *117*

Finding Deep Confidence in God as You Build   *125*

About the Author   *127*

ACKNOWLEDGMENTS

Writing a book is a new endeavor for me. As I worked through the process, so many faces and names came to mind, of people who have helped in direct and indirect ways. I'm humbled to see how kind God has been!

Going way back, my mom and dad prayed as they worked their way through sixty-two years of marriage, raising a family along the way. Dad loved the Bible, and Mom loved the Lord, which was a good combination. No family is perfect, but I'm grateful for mine and their constant love.

Lloyd, thank you for your love and support. I'm glad we're opposites, as you have strengths where I'm weak. Your knack for providing opportunities along the way has made me grow and think more broadly. Being married to you and raising a family together have been among my favorite parts of life.

My kids cheer me on and inspire me to keep learning and adapting as I get older. I love my grandkids, and the unique ways my kids have lived out their commitment to them and to their spouses. Thanks for encouraging me to write this book.

Specific to this book, I have to say thanks to the team at HIM Publications: Chad Harrington, Molly Crowson, and Christy Nicholson in editing; and Bryana Anderle in design. They added improvements and professionalism every step of the way. They are great to work with—thank you all!

My friends who proofread this book are worth their weight in gold. Thank you, Liza Williams, Leslie Pitt, Marieke Desmond, Wendy Hayhoe, Jenna Worsham, Cindy Maurer, and Colleen Peace, for your good work and encouragement.

From my extended family to my life group and church buddies, thank you for believing in this project. Please continue to pray that God will use it to bless many families.

And finally, to all you moms who have attended MomsMentoring groups locally during the last fifteen years and inspired me to take this topic seriously—thank you. I've loved all the great times we've had together so far, learning about things that matter in our marriages and parenting. Here's to you for all the ways you've shared your hearts and lives with me!

INTRODUCTION

Fifteen years ago, four of my friends went through the pain of divorce. As I encountered the fallout—the pain of the adults and children involved—I could feel sadness and anger welling up. A passion to come alongside families in the early years—to support and encourage them in their marriages and parenting—began to grow in me. Around the same time, many people at my church were becoming Jesus-followers and wanted to develop faith-based marriages and families. There were gaps between what these new believers desired and their knowledge of how to implement a new way of living. As someone who grew up in a faith-filled home, I felt a growing desire to come alongside and support young parents step by step on the adventure of being Christians in today's world. Maybe, just maybe, we could be part of helping families build something strong on the front end that would still be standing many years down the road.

The Wise Woman

My friend Beth and I decided to meet with young moms who had lots of questions. We made two lists: one titled "What's Working" and the other "What's Not Working." From those lists a discussion-based curriculum developed, built on what was relevant to the moms. Together, we met to learn and wrestle with what the Bible says about marriage and parenting. Eventually we named our group "MomsMentoring" to reflect the importance of what these moms were doing and to applaud and encourage their efforts. Our theme verse at MomsMentoring became "The wise woman builds her house" (Prov. 14:1, NIV), the keynote verse for this book.

The goal of this book is to extend what we have been learning over the past fifteen years to even more women. As you grow to become a wise mom, working alongside God with intentionality, we cheer you on as you engage in fashioning a home built on Christ—one that is strong and lasting.

Builds Her House

"The wise woman builds her house." Every house has a foundation, walls, an interior, a roof, windows, and doors. Each are important for the house to function well. Unlike building a physical house, we get to practice as we go, learning together how a strong foundation built on God's love and wisdom supports the marriage relationship and the formation of the children under your roof. Like windows and doors give us access to the world outside our homes, our interactions with others provide us access to the broader culture we live in.

I'm going to assume that you are building your home based on the wisdom of the Bible, a living relationship with Jesus, and good-sized doses of Holy Spirit help. I believe that God wants to bless families, and while building a home requires effort and intentionality, God is the Master Builder, and we get to partner with him. Others will join us in this endeavor too: friends from our local churches, online encouragers, like-minded friends who are in the same season of life, and older mentors who can love, cheer, and pray for us—all of these will be worth their weight in gold.

No two moms are the same, which makes this world an interesting place. While our parenting styles and life circumstances vary, God wants to work with each of us to build a strong home. If you're a single mom, please know that my heart is for you, and I don't presume to understand all the aspects of your journey. But I am anticipating that God's grace will show up and meet your needs along the way. If you are married, know that your husband will benefit from the discussions that ensue as you read through each chapter.

As you'll see, I'm not writing as an expert. After all, I've only walked this path once myself! But I have been blessed to journey alongside many other women as we have discussed marriage and parenting roles together. So you will get the fruit of what I've learned from them as well.

This is a get-you-started kind of book. It will inspire you to pray, have lively conversations, dig into research, and get even more curious about your life as you decide how to deploy the agency God has given you. Whether you're new to the faith or a veteran, the few minutes or hours it will take you to read this book could change outcomes in your family many years from now.

There are only a few ways to have an unhealthy family, but there are hundreds of different ways to have a good one. It's great fun to learn about how your family can be enjoyable, unique, and a place you just want to be!

How to Use This Book

I recommend beating this book up: take notes, underline, and highlight sections to discuss with your spouse, a group, or a friend. Make it yours!

I also encourage you to access two video series we created to go with this book. These short videos supplement the content of this book. The first video series, called "Wise Moms Readers," aligns with each chapter. It gives you a chance to "meet me" in a more personal way, as well as injecting some fun and encouragement into each of these topics! Visit WiseMomsBook.com/videos to access this series.

The website also includes a series of short videos for *Wise Moms* group leaders called "Wise Moms Leaders," which take you step by step through the book and equips you to lead moms through studying this book together. Whether you're a young mom who wants to meet up with some friends, or an older mom who wants to support and encourage younger moms, the *Wise Moms* leader videos will make it easy for you to lead! Visit WiseMomsBook.com/videos to gain free access to these video series.

The "Make It Yours" section at the end of each chapter uses a "Read, Talk, Plan" format to take you deeper. Use your phone to schedule actions and reminders as you read so you don't have to rack your brain later, trying to remember what you read. Make notes when you find fun topics for date nights, or think of a plan for what you want to do with the content you just read. Finally, include your spouse. This book is geared toward moms, but if you're married, all the topics will be enhanced by your spouse's feedback.

I've enjoyed working with hundreds of moms over the past fifteen years. No two moms are the same, no two marriages are the same, and no two families are the same; I've decided God likes variety. Each family gets to use the agency God has given us to make choices as we embark on this building project. Our circumstances dictate that our situations look different from those of our friends. Having agency means that we have freedom in our circumstances, not freedom from them, and we can make choices that help us build well.

A mom becomes wise over time, so let's start building!

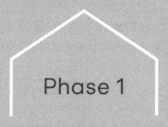

Phase 1

THE FOUNDATION

*A Wise Mom's Connection
with God and Herself*

Who you are as a wife and mom is key to building something solid for those you love. Your relationship with God colors your life every day and influences how you show up in the world and in your family. Feel the excitement as the foundation gets laid, outlining the home you dream of, built on Christ.

Phase Summary

When you pursue an intimate relationship with Jesus, receive blessed by the way he heals, and get on board his wisdom for your marriage and parenting, you are on your way to building a quality foundation!

Chapter 1 affirms that we can start right where we are. God's promises are faithful and true at every stage of our lives. In Chapter 2, our self-esteem gets some honest consideration as we learn how God created us uniquely, and we learn to celebrate ourselves and others. Chapter 3 frees us to be explorers of our own stories and their implications as we create new chapters with our spouses and children. Chapter 4 explores our inner world, looking at the importance of our emotions and the value of partnering with God to convert less-positive emotions into things like patience, positivity, and hopefulness.

1

BUILDING YOUR
HOUSE WITH GOD

Wouldn't it be lovely to feel even more comfortable in our relationships with God? To engage with our world knowing that we are loved by God, precious to him, uniquely one-of-a-kind? To interact with our spouses and children based on a rock-solid self-esteem that gives us joy?

It's easy to compare ourselves with other mothers and feel that we are lacking in this area, and it can be especially unsettling if we're new to faith and have friends with long spiritual journeys that seem far superior to our own.

I remember years ago when Bill and Glynn joined a life group at our home. Bill was a funny guy, and after getting settled, he sat back and asked, "Do you have a *Bible for Dummies*?" He was a brand-new Jesus-follower and was sure he'd ask lots of dumb questions. We all chuckled, but truly their experience with Jesus was so new that they brought a lot of freshness and clarity to our group as we studied and learned together. They were eager to apply what they were learning to their marriage and parenting, and they taught us a lot with their thoughtful questions and openness to letting God reshape their lives.

Everyone is on a level playing field when it comes to a relationship with God. It doesn't matter where anyone comes from, but it is vitally interesting to see where they are going and then join them on their journey. Everyone has a unique relationship with God, so don't worry if your walk with Jesus looks different than someone else's. The pastor at my church has a winsome invitation at the beginning of his talks: "Whether you're curious about Jesus, cautious about Jesus, or committed to Jesus, this is a safe place to be. As long as you don't have it all together, you'll fit right in." I like that.

Some days I feel close to God, and other days, not as much. Looking back over my life, I now can see how patient God has been, how he took his time to teach me, how he brought along encouragement when I was at the end of my rope, and how he sometimes provided people to give me a kick in the seat of my pants and get me going in a new direction.

We often want instant spiritual maturity, but maybe that's why God gives us children—to remind us that our maturity happens step by step, just like theirs. And while we all have many things in common, remember that your life is yours alone. God is intent on meeting you, shaping you, and loving you in a one-of-a-kind way.

My niece Ange wrote a poem about all the transitions she was experiencing during the "young wife and mom" season of her life:

> Along my journey of change, God never pointed off in the distance and said,
>
> "You should be there and not here." No.
>
> That's not how God works. He's met me exactly where I was,

> Walking the road with me like a calm, gentle tour guide.
>
> Slowly, over many ventures
>
> Where he's turned up faithful yet again,
>
> I've learned to follow without question.
>
> The breathtaking views at the end of each one
>
> Are something I've come to wait expectantly for.

Starting Places

The moms I've interacted with have come from so many interesting places. Marie had questions about teaching her children to pray; neither she nor her husband came from a family that prayed, and she was unsure about getting started. Colleen was in a blended family and had a stepson as well as two young children with her husband. She had been a missionary in her earlier life, and while she had a strong biblical foundation, she had practical questions about her role as a stepmom and her relationship with her husband's ex-wife. Some of the moms I met grew up in alcoholic families and were keen to provide something different for their own children. No matter our backgrounds, life requires us to go deeper with Jesus.

No matter our backgrounds, life requires us to go deeper with Jesus.

My sister-in-law Julie has been through lots of good times and hard times during her forty-year marriage. In her family, she has experienced severe health issues, job loss, financial stress, and extended family challenges, along with times when things were peaceful and easier. I have watched God grow and

21

shape her through it all. Julie sent me a note recently, with her reflections on her early life as a wife and mom. Listen in:

> My prayer for your book is that it would point all young moms to Jesus. I wonder what it would mean if every mom that reads your book could look back after twenty years of marriage and realize that God was in each moment, that he was there during the hard times, that any time they tried to make it on their own and failed, he was there. During the lonely times, when it felt like everything was crashing, in every moment that they felt broken and hurt and wanted to give up, that it was actually a blessing and a part of their personal journey to become the person God created them to be!

When all is said and done, the most valuable gift I can give you is to encourage you to seek Jesus. And while you seek Jesus, also ask him to send along a "Julie" for you who can offer support and encouragement.

Letting God Shape Us

When I was a little girl, my mom read Bible stories to us. She wanted to give us a spiritual foundation that included learning the Bible's stories. The interesting thing was, she was often learning the stories herself as she read. They were new to her as well. She was thrilled to be able to provide us with something she hadn't experienced as a child. I'm sure it wasn't always easy to navigate, and she had to be willing to learn from others, but I am so grateful for the example she passed down to me and my sisters.

When we asked her a few years ago what she knew at eighty that she wished she had known when she was younger, she replied,

"Early on, as a new Christian, I learned that God cares about the big things in my life, but I wish I'd known he cares about every little detail and that nothing is too small to pray about."

Where are you in your relationship with God? What would you like more of? A good starting place is honesty. Here's my list: I'd like deeper faith and more discipline in spending daily time with God through reading the Bible and prayer. I'd like to become more loving, less critical, a better listener, and willing to take risks—for starters! I've been on a journey with Jesus for over fifty-five years, and there are still so many ways he is growing me and showing me more of his love. The adventure never ends!

Maybe you're the first one in your clan to be building a marriage and family based on a faith foundation—cheers to you! Jesus is the cornerstone of this building project, and he is unchanging, faithful, loving, patient, and kind. You can trust him with your marriage, and you can trust him with your family.

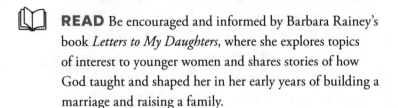

Make It Yours

READ Be encouraged and informed by Barbara Rainey's book *Letters to My Daughters*, where she explores topics of interest to younger women and shares stories of how God taught and shaped her in her early years of building a marriage and raising a family.

TALK If your spouse is open to it, pick a Bible reading plan to do together or separately, and compare notes once a week to discuss what you're learning.

PLAN Download a Bible reading app like YouVersion. The Message is one of my favorite translations—a very readable version of the Bible that aligns with many of the verses in this book. Many Bible apps have marriage and parenting plans that are encouraging and helpful.

2

CELEBRATING MOTHERS OF MANY STYLES

Today's culture, soaked in social media, makes it easy for moms to compare and compete. I chat with women all the time who step away, at least for a time, from online platforms that make them feel diminished as wives and mothers. I wish I'd learned earlier the value of connection and community in my relationships with other moms. Years ago, I had to ask God for his help to corral my ego when it strayed into "I'm better than" or "I'm worse than" patterns of thinking. Practicing "I'm OK, you're OK" as a mantra in my early parenting years would have made me a kinder, more empathetic friend.

Tracey, a mom with one son, told me she was relieved when she stopped comparing herself to her organized neighbor who had four kids and structured routines that kept things mostly on track. Tracey was more random and not as organized. However, she discovered that when plans changed abruptly, she was able to go with the flow, while the mom of four would come somewhat unglued and have a harder time switching to Plan B.

My friend Beth, who has partnered with me at MomsMentoring for many years, has strengths where I'm weak. She's a good listener, a competent behind-the-scenes person, and an administrative whiz. We have been a good team for over a decade as we've had fun serving moms together.

Uniquely You

You can't be every type of person, but there are many ways to be the person God designed you to be. What would it look like to parent based on who God has hardwired you to be and the strengths he's given you? I love Isaiah 64:8: "Yet you, LORD, are our Father. We are the clay, you are the potter; we are all the work of your hand" (NIV). It's freeing to learn your God-given style and sink deeply into who you are, bringing the best of that to your roles as wife and mother.

Years ago, I learned about the Myers-Briggs personality analysis and CliftonStrengths, which identifies your top strengths. I was curious, so I sat down and took the assessments. I learned that as an ESFJ (Extroversion/Sensing/Feeling/Judging), I tend to gain energy by being with people. I process information through my senses, rather than intuitively. My decisions are based more on emotions than analysis, and I prefer structure and planning over figuring things out on the fly. My top strengths are "Input" and "Woo"—I like to research and collect information. While "Woo" sounds like an unusual strength, it stands for "winning others over." I liked the attitude that developed in me as a result of this knowledge—I began thanking God for my strengths, practiced using them well, and became more accepting of areas where I'm not a superstar.

A book called *MotherStyles* by Janet Penley was pivotal in teaching me how to use the Myers-Briggs analysis to discover my parenting strengths. Penley wrote about the changes that happened as she learned about her own wiring:

> My core belief in one "right" way to mother changed and I could begin to see the "rightness" of many different approaches. . . . Knowing my type has helped me manage my personal energy, find a balance between work and play, and stay true to myself in decisions as minor as whether to be room mother for my daughter's fourth-grade class and how much was I willing to travel for work.[1]

It was freeing to learn that I had specific strengths and struggles, just like every other mom. At first, I felt too me-focused spending time learning my strengths, but then I was reminded that strengths are for service, not status. We can use our strengths in a way that supports and encourages other moms, cheering them on.

What if a mom friend is new to faith or nervous about her parenting skills, perhaps feeling shame about some aspect of her life? Or maybe she is very competent, and skilled in areas that we are not. What would it feel like to be happy with who God made us to be while encouraging and celebrating the diversity of other moms who are as different as night and day? That sounds fun! I still tend to be a competitive person, so I remind myself often that

---

1. *MotherStyles: Using Personality Type to Discover Your Parenting Strengths* (Da Capo Lifelong Books, 2006), introduction.

connection and community are far superior to comparing and competing.

Family Benefits

> Connection and community are far superior to comparing and competing.

A huge bonus for me was when my husband, Lloyd, also did the personality assessments. We are opposites in almost every way, but as we learned what makes us tick, we adopted better ways of communicating, managing conflict, and parenting. I learned what Lloyd's strengths were and began to understand how he used them to bless our family in ways that were different from mine. He's an introvert, and his style is distinctive from my extroverted approach to life. I began to develop a new level of appreciation for what he brought to our family.

When my girls graduated from high school, I had a "Many Mothers" party. I invited the ladies who had been influential in my girls' lives, served them dinner, and thanked them for their input into Caroline and Jennie over the years. Each of those women had strengths and talents that differed from mine, and I was thrilled that my girls had been influenced and blessed by a whole cadre of women living out their faith and lives in varied ways.

After our supper with these women, my daughter Jennie, who had spent lots of time in several of their homes, shared that she intended to incorporate aspects of how those families did life into her future home—and she hoped I wouldn't be offended. Not at all—that's how it should be! I knew she would adopt some of how her dad and I did life as well as our friends' lifestyles, while still developing her own unique style. In certain seasons, I was tempted to feel that I had to be all things to my children, and it was freeing to learn that my kids didn't need a perfect mother.

For me, learning to celebrate other moms without feeling pressure to be like them was a slow process. But the more I learned to enjoy God's love for me personally, the easier it became. Now, I love cheering on other moms in this gradual journey toward community rather than comparison.

Make It Yours

 READ I've enjoyed reading the interesting book *Bittersweet* by Shauna Niequist, who transparently shares what she learned in her twenties and early thirties as she worked to understand who God had made her to be. And the book *MothersStyles* by Janet Penley that I mentioned in this chapter was a game changer for me as well!

 TALK Remember, dads all have different styles too. Think about your children's father and his wiring. How can you highlight one of his strengths and offer him empathy? Follow the model of Ephesians 5:22: "Wives, understand and support your husbands in ways that show your support for Christ."

 PLAN Text or call a friend and encourage her today by highlighting some strengths you see in her.

3

UNPACKING YOUR LIFE STORY

Each of us brings a lot to who we are in this moment. Your spiritual journey, family of origin, previous experiences, and education create the foundation of the "who" you are as a spouse and parent. Looking at the factors that have shaped you is a helpful piece of the puzzle as you begin building a strong marriage— or the potential for one—and a Jesus-following family.

Our stories are unique; sometimes they are hard, and all of them have quirky elements. A look back to the past will help you and your spouse decide what you want to pass on to your children and where you see patterns of behavior that you want to relearn. As you reflect on the seasons of your life so far, you may find wonderful things to celebrate, places that need healing, or areas of growth that would be fun to explore.

Celebrating

The stories in the Bible give us many examples of celebrating. King David was good at it! In Psalm 126:2 he said, "We laughed, we sang, we couldn't believe our good fortune. We were the talk of the nations—'GOD was wonderful to them!' GOD *was* wonderful to us; we are one happy people."

As we look back and see God's love and care, our hearts are bolstered for what's to come in the future. Is there an area where you've seen God bless you and you never took the time to celebrate? Is it time to celebrate now?

Sharing these God stories with your children will build a faith foundation in their hearts. One year, we had a bonfire at a family gathering and asked my mom and dad to share stories from when they were young. They shared the story of their faith formation, where they had seen God work in their lives through ups and downs. We then went around the fire and asked each person to share something they were grateful for and something or someone they would like us to pray about. It was a great celebration of how God had worked in my parents' lives. It was not elaborate; it was just a simple bonfire, but it was good.

Pick one thing in your family, big or small, where you see God's hand at work, and celebrate in a way that's meaningful to you!

Healing

I can't think of a single person who isn't in need of some healing. As fallen people in a fallen world, none of us has it all together. Under stress and the enemy's attacks, we will be tempted to default to sinful patterns of behavior. But imagine if we link arms and admit together that we need help outside ourselves at those times. Being able to ask for help is a sign of strength, not weakness.

> *Asking for help is a sign of strength, not weakness.*

Thank God for his healing work in our lives. We can trust him as we take steps in new directions and start building on a firmer foundation than what we experienced in the past. I hope that, like Lloyd and I, you have a Christian counselor on speed dial. If not, perhaps that is your first action step: "Find a Christian counselor near me." Another helpful option to facilitate healing is honest conversations with a trusted spiritual director, friend, or mentor.

One of my biggest challenges during my parenting years was developing panic attacks and anxiety that became quite severe. When they began, I saw a medical doctor, prayed, journaled, and talked with Lloyd. Over time, I found a Christian counselor, who referred me to a psychiatrist. Prozac got added to my daily schedule. You can imagine the unsettledness of this yearlong season. Thankfully, the medication helped me feel like myself again.

I remember thinking at the time how hard it was, how painful. As I slowly recovered, weaned off medications, and worked my way back into "normal life" again, I began to value the shaping God allowed me through that trial. My empathy increased, I learned to be more humble, and I depended more on God instead of myself. New lifestyle patterns emerged for Lloyd and me and our family as we realized that a simpler life was going to be a better choice for my mental well-being.

Whatever your needs are for healing, trust that someday you will be able to read Psalm 30:2 and add your "Amen" to it: "GOD, my God, I yelled for help and you put me together." In my spirit, there was definitely some yelling going on as God did his work on his timetable, not mine! I can remember praying for patience, but somehow I didn't expect this particular situation to be the way I practiced learning it.

Learning

As you read through this book, think about where you want to develop this year, and embrace the fun of learning in that area. Suppose you discover your family is not as familiar with the Bible as you wish: you can enjoy finding a whole world of entertaining ways to make Bible stories come alive to you and your kids. Building community at church means you'll meet moms who can pass ideas and resources along as their children move up in years. I never met a hand-me-down book that I didn't love!

What a privilege to learn new ways of doing and being that allow us to teach positive family behaviors, like transforming less productive emotions into positive ones. If you never saw good conflict management modeled well in your family of origin, you will have some great decisions to make. You can find additional help by learning with books, blogs, and videos or signing up for a study at church or in your life group—so many fun choices!

Learning and growing means we don't have to default to negative ways of doing life with our families. We can celebrate what was good about our families of origin while exercising agency in making new choices for here and now.

The Book of Your Life

Let's pretend we're each writing a book about our life. Some of my chapters would be:

- Happy Childhood Days
- Wobbly Teenage Faith
- The Twenties: An Early Start as Mr. & Mrs. and Mom & Dad

- Panic Attacks: Will There Ever Be Anything Good to Say About This Season?
- College/Weddings/Grandbabies: How Did I Get Here So Fast?

Looking back on my life to this point, I have more clarity on some of the good God brought out of even the hard times. My childhood was relatively smooth sailing, but sooner or later, things happen in life that cause us to have some honest conversations with God. I'm glad he can handle it! Making my faith my own felt like a scary season as I wrestled with apologetic questions that demanded answers. It took a while to make my faith my own.

I grew up in Canada and met my husband, Lloyd, when we were kids. He grew up in the US, but his cousins went to our church. When they came to visit in the summer, this interesting family with four boys caught the attention of a Canadian girl, who had only sisters! Canada became Lloyd's home too during our early years of marriage and raising three children. Our farm near Ottawa was a great play place for our kids, and I enjoyed being a stay-at-home mom and helping Lloyd with our family business. Our daughter Caroline was diagnosed with a rare growth condition when she was two, so we spent many years traveling to Ohio, where she was part of a clinical trial. That experience stretched our faith muscles; we had no guaranteed outcomes, which felt scary. Thirteen years later when the treatment turned out to be beneficial, and the government approved the drug to help other children with growth disorders, we pulled out all the stops on a grand celebration.

After twelve years in Canada, the cold weather began to wear Lloyd down. Following a lot of prayer and planning, we moved to the US, and North Carolina has been home for the last thirty years. It was exciting but challenging to move to a place where we didn't know anyone. A few years later, panic attacks became part of my reality, forcing new learning on multiple levels. To my surprise, the times in my life that have been the hardest have been when I've felt deeply loved by God, which has taught me not to be so quick to call good things "good" or bad things "bad."

Now it's your turn to think about your life so far and how you would title your chapters! Whether on your phone or with pen and paper, write down what they would be. For each one, ask yourself:

- Is there something I need to celebrate?
- Is there anything that needs healing?
- Do I see any areas where I need to grow and learn?

As you go through your own chapters of life, choose one to take action with, whether it's celebrating, healing, or learning. After you identify a step you want to take, insert that action into your calendar.

No book can give you all the answers for your life. As you come to see that only God understands all the myriad details of time, relationships, and circumstances, your trust in God has the opportunity to grow. Being guided by prayer, the Bible's teachings, the Holy Spirit's nudging, and God's daily wisdom is the only way I know to make it through.

Make It Yours

 READ *One Thousand Gifts* by Ann Voskamp uniquely details the story of one woman's journey into a relationship with Jesus, and how that played out in her marriage and family.

 TALK Ask your spouse what he sees as celebration-worthy in your family. How would he enjoy celebrating that?

 PLAN On your phone, schedule a date night or couch chat when you can share with your spouse the chapter titles of the book about your life so far. Ask your husband to write his as well. Together, identify where healing or growing would benefit your marriage and family, and schedule a first step to take in that direction.

4

MANAGING YOUR
EMOTIONS

In this season of life, do you feel as if you're managing your
emotions or being managed by them? Since you're a mother
with children, I'm guessing some of each! For me, living with my
spouse and kids gave me plenty of opportunities to be sweet and
loving one moment and filled with anger and anxiety the next.
Our emotions are a gift from God; they add richness and color to
our lives, and they also warn us of danger. And as parents, we set
the emotional tone in our homes.

Sometimes we discover that we are in need of emotional
healing or learning, or both. A Christian friend of mine went
to Emotions Anonymous when her children were young. When
she was a child, her emotions had been squashed or dismissed
by her parents, and she had a hard time knowing how to even
name what she was feeling. I was so proud of her for the work she
did to create an environment where her own kiddos would learn
the value of positive emotions and have faith-based help to identify and work through negative emotions. In our fallen world,
we need God's help every day to navigate the impact of emotions that threaten to undo us and our families. The Bible is our

guidebook for managing our emotions. It is often a long process that takes place over many years, but we have the promise of the Holy Spirit's help.

Emotional Challenges

One of the ways God helped me early in my marriage was through a book by Joyce Meyers called *Living Beyond Your Feelings*. This book gave me a deeper understanding of how powerful emotions are in our lives. Meyers helped me learn the value of talking with God before I talked to Lloyd about things that were bothering me. I remember times when I felt angry and would march to our bedroom and shut the door with gusto. In the privacy of my room, I'd admit to God how I was feeling. I knew that dealing well with what was bothering me meant I needed to stay in there until I'd had time to talk with God about it and let myself calm down. Trying to resolve issues while my emotions were running high would not help build a strong foundation for my family's house. Instead, it would put me in danger, through my hasty, angry words, of tearing down the very foundation I was trying to construct.

My friend Lisa found the early parenting years challenging and would easily default to yelling at her kids. She wanted to change that, and one of the tools she used was to ask a friend to hold her accountable. Her friend checked in every Monday morning and asked, "How did it go?" It helped Lisa to know that someone cared and was in her corner cheering her on. Lisa also learned to accept that, due to the personalities and culture of her family, her household was always going to be lively, spirited, and loud. Once she understood that her personality style was bold and forthright, and that God made her to be that unique person and mom, she was able to stop comparing herself to more quiet-mannered moms. Lisa's lively, bouncy presence adds zest to any gathering, and I'm glad God made her the way she is!

Sometimes a walk or other types of self-care can help when things get tense at home. However, when you have young children and can't easily get out of the house, talking to God in your bedroom is a first-rate way to push the reset button! Singing praise songs always reminded me of God's love, even in the middle of difficult family situations. Reminders of his care and presence take some of the sting out of the pain you experience when things are not going well.

While we can work to manage our own emotions, we can't control the emotions of other people. I love how God can be a shield for me when I spend time with people who aren't skilled at managing their emotions. Psalm 18:1–2 describes this protection with a comforting illustration: "I love you, GOD—you make me strong. GOD is bedrock under my feet, the castle in which I live, my rescuing knight. My God—the high crag where I run for dear life, hiding behind the boulders, safe in the granite hideout." Sometimes during our interactions with others, we need to "run for dear life" to God. Only he can protect and buffer us from the fallout of the negative emotions we face on a daily basis.

> Only God can protect us from the fallout of negative emotions.

Boundaries for Healthy Interactions

Many moms wonder how to show honor while setting healthy boundaries with parents or in-laws who are challenging to get along with. The Bible instructs us to honor our parents. Does that mean spending large amounts of time with people who are detrimental to the well-being of our families? Brainstorm with your spouse how it could look to be creative In this area. Pray for God's love to be the driving force undergirding all of your family relationships, even if other family members are not believers. Showing love in tangible ways to hard-to-love people, while maintaining healthy boundaries, may be one of the biggest ways you model for your children what it looks like to follow and obey the Lord.

In 1 Corinthians 13:4–5 the Bible shows what loving, healthy interaction is like when it says:

> Love cares more for others than for self.
> Love doesn't want what it doesn't have.
> Love doesn't strut,
> Doesn't have a swelled head,
> Doesn't force itself on others,
> Isn't always "me first,"
> Doesn't fly off the handle,
> Doesn't keep score of the sins of others.

Insert yourself into this verse, and ask if this sentence is true of you. For me, is it true that Linda is unselfish, isn't always "me first," doesn't keep score of the sins of others? Lloyd would be a very fortunate man if I committed to living out that verse with God's help!

James 1:19 says, "Lead with your ears, follow up with your tongue, and let anger straggle along in the rear." I witnessed this firsthand, as my mom didn't grow up in a Christian family, and she had a lively temper. After she became a Christian, she wrote out some verses like the one above, and we'd see them beside the phone or tucked into the window frame above the kitchen sink. She was determined to change her patterns of behavior with God's help. If you met her today, at eighty-six, you'd never dream that she was once that person. I was blessed by her efforts to partner with the Holy Spirit in his slow but steady work of transformation.

Future Focus

We are impacted by where we came from, but where we're going is what we can focus on now. Maybe you grew up in a family with lots of judgment or comparison. Perhaps envy and jealousy were regular emotions in your home. How exciting to learn a new way of living that, bit by bit, means your children grow up in a very different home from the one you were raised in! Share with some friends an area where you're trying to unlearn old habits and learn new ways of managing your emotions, and ask what books or resources have been helpful to them.

Use your phone to record your thoughts or write your intentions on your calendar as you read through the following questions:

1. A healthy family begins with your emotional wellness. To what degree are you willing to begin reading books or get professional Christian help for areas in your life that you know need healing, such as depression, perfectionism, trauma, anger, or postpartum depression?
2. We all have emotional deficits because we are human. How do you plan to grow in areas where you didn't see healthy emotions modeled well? Will you tackle those issues through a class, a podcast, or a book? When you engage with a

resource, confirm that the author's viewpoint aligns with the Bible's teachings.

3. Can you identify people you can connect with for emotional support and accountability as you do this work? Ask God to provide people who are safe and trustworthy and who can keep what you share confidential.

4. Since healthy emotions are such a blessing, how can you celebrate all the good ones that God has blessed you with?

Make It Yours

 READ Check out *Living Beyond Your Feelings* by Joyce Meyers. I learned a ton about managing my emotions from this book, and it also tackles topics about emotional trauma.

 TALK Ask your husband for his input. Select a resource to help you each continue to grow in this area. Check in with each other once a week, with a simple question: "How's it going?"

 PLAN Use your phone to write out Bible verses that encourage you to use your words carefully. They make good screen savers! A good one to start with is Ephesians 4:29: "Watch the way you talk. Let nothing foul or dirty come out of your mouth. Say only what helps, each word a gift."

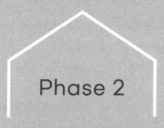

Phase 2

THE WALLS AND ROOF

A Wise Mom's Connection with Her Spouse

You are a builder! If you're married, you have a co-builder, who also has ideas for what your home should be like. The enthusiasm you feel as you see the walls go up and the shingles getting hammered in place can get dampened when you bump up against your spouse's vision for the project. Becoming competent co-builders is a learning curve for you both.

Phase Summary

The walls of a house grow upward and contain the spaces where your family practices, grows, and thrives. As we partner with God and follow his blueprints, our marriages begin to grow and thrive too.

In Chapter 5 we'll look at prioritizing our marriages and keeping them at the center of our family lives. Chapter 6 explores ways to keep our love alive during the busy years of raising a family.

Chapter 7 covers the important topic of learning Bible-based communication and conflict-management skills to build strong walls of protection against the toxic effects of harsh words. And in Chapter 8 we'll look at how some of the upside-down teachings of the Bible might be more right-side-up than we think!

It's exciting when the rooms of a house start to take shape. It's the beginning of something that, laid on a firm foundation, can stand the test of time, creating something solid for generations to come.

5

BUILDING A MARRIAGE-CENTERED FAMILY

I s your family child-centered or marriage-centered? Why does it matter? I've been asking moms that question for the past fifteen years. There are moments or seasons when a child has special needs and is center stage, and rightfully so. But building a family that, overall, is marriage-centered will provide the structure everyone needs to weather life's storms.

Lloyd and I were out for a walk with our kids when they were about ten, eight, and five. Lloyd is an introvert and usually doesn't talk until he's thought something through. As we were strolling along, he said, "Linda, I think if you invested half as much energy into our marriage as you do into the kids, our marriage would be humming."

What? Where did that come from? I thought our marriage was humming! I was mad and hurt.

Lloyd went on: "Don't get me wrong; you're a great mom. You pay attention to the kids, and you think about and plan for what they need mentally, physically, emotionally, spiritually, and socially. It's just that sometimes I feel second." His commendation of my mothering skills offset some of my anger, and he had a plaintive tone to his voice when he mentioned feeling second. I knew I had some thinking and praying to do.

A common time for people to get divorced is after their youngest child leaves for college. That's startling, and it can affect any of us, even those of us with faith-based families. I loved my husband and knew I wanted a marriage worth celebrating after the children left home. After Lloyd shared his observation, my mind flew back to a conversation I had with a friend who hosted a baby shower for me when my first baby, Carter, was born. Mary Jane said, "Make sure you stay friends with your husband. You don't want to sit across the breakfast table from him twenty-five years from now and ask yourself, 'Who is this guy?'"

At the time, I thought her comment was hilarious. That would never happen—we were young, in love, and had our first adorable baby. But Mary Jane was twenty years ahead of me and knew something I didn't about how spouses can easily drift apart without being intentional. My mothering role was important and was where I invested most of my thinking and energy, but it was time to consider the bigger picture of my life, not just my role as a mom.

After thinking, praying, and having more conversations, Lloyd and I both made some changes. We started learning how to have crucial conversations; we read books about becoming soul-mates, not just roommates; and we talked with the kids about our marriage being central, with them as "welcome additions." Bit by bit, we read books about love languages, listened to podcasts, read articles, and did Bible studies with friends who were all committed to learning in these same areas. We became more intentional and creative about carving out time when we could relax and have fun together.

Early Learning

It suited our budget to get a pizza on Tuesday nights—the $5.99 special back then. We'd head to the local park overlooking a lake, and Lloyd and I would sit the kids at a picnic table and eat our own pizza slices on a bench 100 yards away. It was great. The kids could be kids, and we didn't have to hear them. They would roar around on their rollerblades afterward while we relaxed and took our time, enjoying the view and the chance for some adult-only conversation. We told the kids not to talk to us unless they were bleeding!

In our early parenting years, I had shifted gears, moving from working full-time in a dental office to being at home. As Lloyd was working hard in his role as a real-estate developer, I put out genuine effort in my role as a mom and gave it my best shot. Looking back, we can see how easy it was for us both to get a little lopsided in our priorities. We didn't intend to drift apart, but without some intentionality it happens easily enough on its own!

Maybe you can relate to this in your marriage. Especially when communication is challenging, it can be easier to just get good at doing the mechanics of life together, without deeply connecting at a soul or spiritual level. Some couples find it helpful to pray together each day or in a rhythm that works for them.

Brainstorm what makes you feel connected with each other and think of creative ways to fit it into your life. Even "now and then" deep connection can go a long way to building the "us-ness" of your marriage. Think about how your phone can be helpful in this area. There's no shame in scheduling "us" time, even if it's fifteen minutes after work to connect and be together before family dinner and evening activities begin. One friend mentioned that her husband calls her on his way home from work and talks about his day. That way, he has an easier time shifting into family mode when he walks through the door.

It's fun to learn what makes your unique family function well. Lloyd is at his best when he's in a tidy environment with a lower level of chaos. I had to choose either to be resentful about picking up things so he could come home to a tidy house or to do that as a gift to him. Over time, God softened my heart so I could, with the children's help, offer this as a gift. It turned out to be a gift to me. When Lloyd could relax in his surroundings and not feel overwhelmed, he played with the kids and was lively and fun; he helped with the family activities, and a good time was had by all. What seemed like a sacrifice on my part turned out to be a blessing to all.

Colossians 3 is one of my favorite chapters about family relationships, and it has some lovely verses. Read the whole chapter to get the context, but here are some highlights from verses 18 to 20. God cares about our family lives and promises his help and encouragement!

> *Wives*, understand and support your husbands by submitting to them in ways that honor the Master. *Husbands*, go all out in love for your wives. Don't take advantage of them. *Children*, do what your parents tell you. This delights the Master no end.

Kids know when their parents cherish each other. There's safety in that.

I believe the safest place to grow up is in a marriage-centered family. Kids know when their parents cherish each other. There's safety in that. It's healthy for them to know that the world does not circle around them, that they have a place where they belong in the family—but it's not the center!

Kids will learn that your marriage is central to your family and they are welcome additions. This was a long but steady process for us, and over time I could see the walls of our family growing stronger. Our children are now grown with their own families, and we get to see more clearly the benefit of having them be welcome additions while our marriage stayed front and center. It's a joy to be grandparenting together and to see our kids learning to prioritize their spouses and be open to help outside themselves. And they all enjoy when we take the grandkids so they can have quality time with their spouses!

Thought-Provoking Questions

Sometimes questions are more helpful than answers, so here are some thought-provoking questions to discuss with your spouse. Would your marriage be better served:

- If there were no TVs or cellphones in your bedroom? As moms, we often spend lots of time getting a playroom organized for our kiddos. What if we put a similar effort into making our bedrooms a safe, welcoming, and enjoyable space for us and our spouses?
- If you learned each other's love languages? What about making a weekly, recurring note in your calendar to remind you to show love in a way that is meaningful to your spouse? When Lloyd notices my efforts and offers encouragement, his affirming words get my attention, and he loves when I spend time hanging out with him while he washes the car or watches a football game.

- If you scheduled time together as a couple? Brainstorm with your spouse about creative ideas to make time together fun, even if you're on a tight budget.
- If you grabbed your calendar, and blocked off time each week to be together without the kids, and stuck some of these discussion questions into those calendar appointments? If your spouse travels a lot, have a phone date together at a time that works for both of you. If evenings are your low-energy time, try another time, even if you have to let a kids' movie or TV show be a temporary babysitter. The most important step is to set up the time and repeat it regularly.

Prioritizing your marriage with questions like these will prevent you from looking across the kitchen table when the last child leaves home and wondering what you now have in common.

Make It Yours

 READ *Sacred Influence* by Gary Thomas and *The Meaning of Marriage* by Timothy Keller with Kathy Keller are two books that have helped Lloyd and me get reoriented when we need a marriage refresher.

 TALK Discuss with a friend how she and her husband balance their roles as both spouses and parents. Encourage each other to keep making your marriages a priority.

 PLAN Visit WiseMomsBook.com/videos, find the "Wise Moms Readers" series, and watch "Sunday Night Meeting" to hear how one family has Sunday night meetings to keep their marriage front and center. While this amount of planning may not work for you and your spouse, discuss how you could take the idea and apply it in a way that does.

6

KEEPING YOUR
LOVE ALIVE

Lloyd was challenged by his mentor many years ago to make two lists: one of the things in his life that were valuable and the second of the things that were priceless. Then he asked him to write what he was doing to protect the items on both lists. He discovered that his long list of valuable things was largely protected, while the shorter one of priceless things was not.

Keeping love alive between us and within the family is on our priceless list, so committing to learning and practicing these skills has been a way we've chosen to protect what matters most to us. Lloyd and I know that having heart-to-heart conversations is a learned skill and takes practice and courage. I love that Lloyd and I have learned to talk about anything—even the hard stuff. These talks set the standard for every other aspect of our marriage and family life. Watch the "knee-to-knee" video in the "Wise Moms Readers" series at WiseMomsBook.com/videos to see one interesting and fun way of taking baby steps in this area.

Along the Way

When Lloyd coaches people at midlife through his work at the Halftime Institute, he asks them to share their stories. If the person's parents are divorced, that life experience is usually where they begin. Whether the divorce happened when they were age six or eighteen or thirty-three, it's the starting point. Your kids will be given something *priceless* if you and your spouse, with God's help, frame up a way of living that enables your marriage to continue to grow and thrive during the high-energy years of raising those kids.

It's easy during those busy years to let discontentment, comparison, resentment, bitterness, anger, and blame get built into the family structure. Over time, like termites, those things eat away at the walls of our lives. My friend Leslie, a family counselor, taught me that when I experience those types of things, or a sense of disconnect—feeling unseen or unheard—using "I need" statements without implying that my spouse has failed is a powerful skill to learn. *How can I share when I'm angry or overwhelmed in a way that makes Lloyd feel appreciated, loved, and respected?* Maybe you are quick at learning this skill, which is great. But I have been practicing it for a long time, and I continue to see how some affirmation at the beginnings and ends of these conversations can go a long way, as well as choosing a time when my emotions are not running high.

Memorizing Bible verses specific to this life season is key. I love Proverbs 31:10–12: "A good woman is hard to find, and worth far more than diamonds. Her husband trusts her without reserve, and never has reason to regret it. Never spiteful, she treats him generously all her life long." It's hard to treat with generosity a spouse who has sinned against us, until we recollect all the ways we appreciate that same grace coming our way, despite all our quirks and shortcomings!

Your Words

It's not always what we say but how we say it that matters. Much of keeping love alive is about the words that come out of our mouths! Proverbs 18:21 cuts to the heart of it: "Words kill, words give life; they're either poison or fruit—you choose." What would it feel like if you overheard your hubby telling someone that he feels admired by you, appreciated by you, and accepted for who he is? I've been pretty good at criticism all my life, so it's the work of a lifetime for me to continue to grow in this area of encouragement and affirmation.

Ask yourself whether you are willing to compliment your husband and give him credit. Can you accept that only God can meet all your needs? Does your husband have space and time to grow and change? Can you adapt to and adopt some of his preferences? You know what brings out a glow in your husband— use your calendar to remind yourself to do something that puts a smile on his face, and set it as a recurring reminder.

Your Sex Life

Another thing that helps keep your love alive and will definitely put a smile on a husband's face is a good sex life. God designed sex to be a cementing force in a healthy marriage. If you grew up in a family that didn't teach you a positive view of God's design for sexual intimacy, or if you feel that you would benefit from healing past hurts in this area, please

> *God designed sex to be a cementing force in a healthy marriage.*

make that investment and get connected to a good Christian counselor whom you feel comfortable with. I'm convinced that a loving sexual relationship is a key factor that helps keep a marriage strong over a lifetime, through all the ups and downs.

A few years ago, I heard a mom with young children, when discussing how often she and her husband have sex, say that they decided on every four days. Those mornings he'd leave for work with a smile on his face, saying, "It's day four!" After supper, she would head to a bath, relax, and play some nice music. He cleaned up supper, played with the children, and got them off to bed.

This mutual plan worked well for them, but this isn't a blueprint for everyone. Another friend mentioned that she and her husband put a reminder on their calendar so they wouldn't forget to have sex. Sometimes talking about sex with your spouse feels like a big challenge, but having intentional chats about this important topic will help you discover what works best for you at different seasons.

Nonsexual affection is a boon to a marriage as well. A goodbye kiss, a hello kiss, a hug, a smile, or holding hands: all ways to add a little sugar to each day. The little people in your home are picking that up too and often want to join in the fun!

Your Energy

As moms, there are times when, due to feeling overwhelmed or exhausted, this can all feel like "too much." Finding any time to spend with your husband, much less intimate time with him, can seem impossible. It's tempting to think you can focus on the kids now and deal with the marriage later. But the early "building" years of a family are followed by the "maintenance" years, and before you know it, you're raising preteens and teens.

How you manage your schedule to find time with your spouse depends on how you're wired. I've known moms who put their kids to bed in their clothes for the next day, others who partnered with a neighbor to cook twice as much, half as often. During a busy season when our kids were younger, Lloyd and I wrote down all the "good" things we were involved in and gave each one a score of one to ten. Before we began, we agreed that we were going to cut the three lowest-scoring activities, maybe not forever, but for a time. It helped us regain some sanity in a busy season, but it was challenging to do because they were all "good" things. Sometimes the good is the enemy of the best!

Some families set limits on extracurricular programs, and others decide to create fun activities at home so they're not always tempted to be on the go. By building a love-filled home in these current years, you'll find yourself in a love-filled home when the children leave—not a home that's perfect, not one that never has to "rupture and repair," but one where the parents' love for each other was, and is, visible and celebrated. Ruptures in a family are a guaranteed part of living on planet Earth, but repairs are centered in extending love and forgiveness to our spouses and children. It's fun to build a home where the phrases "I'm sorry" and "I forgive you" are part of the glue that holds things together.

Make It Yours

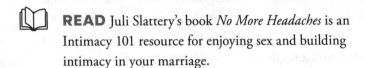 **READ** Juli Slattery's book *No More Headaches* is an Intimacy 101 resource for enjoying sex and building intimacy in your marriage.

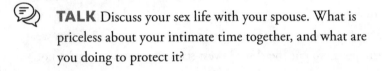 **TALK** Discuss your sex life with your spouse. What is priceless about your intimate time together, and what are you doing to protect it?

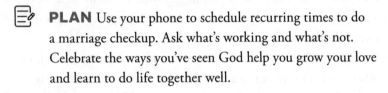 **PLAN** Use your phone to schedule recurring times to do a marriage checkup. Ask what's working and what's not. Celebrate the ways you've seen God help you grow your love and learn to do life together well.

7

LEARNING COMMUNICATION AND CONFLICT MANAGEMENT

A lot of pressure gets relieved when family members can be direct with each other and learn the skill of having crucial conversations. When I am criticized, my first response is to feel resentful and angry, and I want to lash out or at least defend myself. Over time I have learned to see constructive feedback as a helpful tool, as something of a gift. As I make it safe for those around me to point out my blind spots, this allows me to hear well from the people who love me most and are most affected by those blind spots.

Asking myself some questions has proved helpful as I've learned to communicate and manage conflict effectively. Here are a few that I hope will serve you well:

- Is it safe for your spouse to give you feedback?
- When you disagree, do you handle conflict productively?

- Are your children learning the balance of communicating emotions while being respectful and not using their tongues to hurt others?
- Do you "just have to endure" conflict, or can you learn to let crucial conversations actually take you to a better place?

Kids who see Bible-influenced communication and conflict-management skills modeled well develop habits that will be useful in their own families down the road.

Years ago Lloyd and I had a disagreement pattern that went something like this: I'd be stewing about something Lloyd had said or done . . . or not done! I'd finally confront him, expecting to discuss and settle it right then and there. I'd often be teary-eyed because I felt emotional about it. Lloyd felt unprepared for these encounters. Being an introvert, he felt unable to respond because he wanted to think it through first, so he'd back away, and there would be tension and silence between us, sometimes for several days. Eventually we'd talk about it and work on resolving the issue.

That pattern made us reluctant to deal with disagreements because it was painful. Over time we learned a different way to handle conflict. When something was bugging me, I would write it down and put it in my top drawer, then wait a day or two and pray about it. After my emotions subsided and I was thinking more clearly, I pulled out the paper, read it again, and asked myself: When I wrote this, was I tired or hungry or experiencing PMS? If not, is it something I should overlook—"Love makes up for practically anything" (1 Pet. 4:8)—or is it something that is creating a disconnect in the relationship and needs to be addressed? Is this something that will matter twenty years from now?

If the issue truly needed to be addressed, I'd send an email to Lloyd, sans tears and emotion, describing my thoughts. Then I'd wait, sometimes for a couple of days. By then, when Lloyd responded to my concerns, I got his best thinking. He cared about my concerns but needed the freedom to address them in a way that worked for him.

As crazy as it may sound, this worked for us and brought us closer together. I wanted quick answers and solutions, but I had to give up insisting that our rupture and repair happened on my timeline. The Bible says that words kill, especially angry ones. By not spewing angriness in the heat of high emotions, I avoided the serious consequences that come from angry words. I learned patience as I waited, not engaging in the silent treatment or stuffing down resentments, but trusting and asking God to work in both our hearts.

You don't need to copy this style of relating, but you do need to do the work of thinking deeply about how you and your spouse relate. How could you adjust your conflict management in a way that's aligned with the Bible's teachings to bring you to a better place? How can you model for your kids that while conflict will be with us every day of our lives, it doesn't need to undo us? Let me just say that conflict is part of our lives, but it does *not* need to undo us.

Safe Conversations

What would it look like for you and your spouse to have safe conversations about this topic? As two different people with different needs, opinions, ideas, and ways of solving problems, you will need courage and finesse. Practice asking

> Conflict is part of our lives, but it does not *need to undo us.*

open-ended questions with your spouse, and discuss what kind of things were swept under the rug in the home where you grew up. How did people respond to criticism and feedback? Look for the backstories that will help you understand the patterns you default to when you react the way you do. With your spouse, come up with a game plan for how you want to practice handling disagreements, learning to respond rather than react. Pray and ask God for his help as you try to create something that works for you both. You'll gain understanding together by identifying the issues, seeing each other's perspective, and practicing asking good, open-ended questions.

One of the moms at MomsMentoring shared that she and her husband used a scale of one to ten to determine how important something was to each of them when they were having a hard time agreeing. If a spouse cared at a level of three, and the other spouse cared at a level of eight, the decision prioritized the person with the higher number. That idea has been helpful to Lloyd and me when we're not seeing eye to eye!

Listening vs. Speaking

An important part of communication is learning to listen well. I will be working on those skills all my life because listening attentively doesn't come naturally to me. When I'm speaking, I have to remind myself to make sure the conversation is a two-way street. Look at the following listening and speaking habits to identify areas where you want to grow.

INEFFECTIVE LISTENING HABITS	EFFECTIVE LISTENING HABITS
• Assuming you know what the other person is going to say and tuning out • Thinking about your response instead of deeply listening • Jumping in and interrupting	• Waiting for the other person to finish speaking instead of jumping in • Listening actively by echoing back what you hear • Silencing internal distractions, such as being preoccupied with your own thoughts
INEFFECTIVE SPEAKING HABITS	EFFECTIVE SPEAKING HABITS
• Offering solutions before hearing someone out • Jumping to conclusions and putting words in their mouth • Monopolizing the conversation	• Listening more than you talk • Asking open-ended questions, not rhetorical ones • Asking about the other person's perspective

I love how the Bible doesn't pull any punches when it comes to describing our speech, like in James 3:7–10:

> This is scary: You can tame a tiger, but you can't tame a tongue—it's never been done. The tongue runs wild, a wanton killer. With our tongues we bless God our Father;

> with the same tongues we curse the very men and women he made in his image. Curses and blessings out of the same mouth!

Our families are blessed when we learn how to have kind conversations. Some of this is skill-based, combined with the direction and help that comes from the Holy Spirit. Addressing the challenging topics that come up in every family takes practice and courage.

As our kids got married and new members joined our clan, we were grateful for the communication advice we had read and listened to over the years. Over time, God's Spirit transforms old patterns and behaviors. When you need to unlearn and relearn communication patterns, I'd encourage you to seek out books and videos about listening skills and speaking habits. What a gift to your kids if, in their twenties and thirties, they have family members who love each other deeply and have learned to communicate and handle conflict well. Even if it involved the cost of getting professional Christian counseling, it would be money well spent!

Make It Yours

 READ *Crucial Conversations* by Joseph Grenny, Kerry Patterson, and others is a book that has been helpful to both Lloyd and me. The subtitle is *Tools for Talking When Stakes Are High*. Sounds like everyday family life! *Starting Your Marriage Right* by Dennis and Barbara Rainey has helpful, short chapters that apply biblical teaching to mitigate conflict in multiple areas of married life.

 TALK Ask a friend for any podcasts or books that have been helpful to them in this area.

 PLAN Send your spouse a date-night invitation (even if it's on the couch or around a bonfire in the backyard), to begin this conversation about how you have conversations! Small steps make good beginnings.

8

CONSIDERING SUBMISSION—A BIBLE PARADOX

Ever have a sneaking suspicion God knows more about us humans than we do? Some things in the Bible seem upside-down at first glance—like the advice that says if we want to be great, we should be the servant of all, or it is more blessed to give than receive. Sounds upside-down to me!

The paradoxes in the Bible fascinate me. Some things certainly don't seem to make sense at first reading. But I have a new respect for them, and for their impact on family life, after decades of observing my life when I follow these teachings and when I don't. As your family grows, you will have lots of opportunities to discuss how being a Jesus follower influences your choices and decisions. Good things happen when we encourage rather than avoid these invaluable conversations.

One paradox in the Bible involves the topic of submitting to your spouse. The Bible mentions submitting to God, to the authorities in our countries, to our bosses, and to our spouses. Why and how could this be a building block for building your home on Christ? Could it be that your role as a wife could be enhanced, not diminished, by understanding what the Bible teaches about this?

In our culture, there is a cringe factor when we talk about submitting to our spouses. This chapter is a gentle dare for you to stay open about this topic, to reflect deeply on what God is saying and why, and to try it for yourself.

You Bring the Strength!

Colossians 3:18 says, "Wives, understand and support your husbands by submitting to them in ways that honor the Master." Submission is not about who is more important in a marriage; rather both partners are called to honor and serve each other. God designed a husband and wife as equals but allowed for distinctive roles within that equality. When your husband is called to lead his family well, that is a big calling and one that requires a fair amount of help. In the Bible, the Holy Spirit is often referred to as a "helper" (for example, John 14:26, NKJV). We all know the Holy Spirit is no weak-kneed member of the Trinity, as he provides the help that we each need.

> Submission is about both partners honoring and serving each other.

When a woman chooses an attitude of helpfulness, her influence isn't diminished but enhanced. A domineering woman uses her influence to undercut her husband and prove her way is better. What if, instead, we invest our God-given influence to build our husbands' ability to lead? Our culture uses words like "weak," "inferior," or "less-than" when defining submission. Is there a benefit to Christian women reframing those words and developing a willingness to learn the art of adapting, undergirding, and blending? I think so!

As your husband learns to lead his family, he will need your encouragement to live counterintuitively, putting others' needs ahead of his own. Ephesians 5:21–25 provides the blueprint:

> Out of respect for Christ, be courteously reverent to one another. Wives, understand and support your husbands in ways that show your support for Christ. The husband provides leadership to his wife the way Christ does to his church, not by domineering but by cherishing. . . . Husbands, go all out in your love for your wives, exactly as Christ did for the church—a love marked by giving, not getting.

With God's help and a strong woman honoring and supporting him, your husband is much more likely to bring his best. Together, as you develop your unique strengths in the family, with patience, grace, and lots of love, you help each other flourish. This is key to developing a family life that is a source of stability and blessing to your family and to the community around you.

A husband will often, over time, step into servant leadership in areas that he might otherwise shrink from if his leadership attempts are met with scorn or criticism. Leading is a big risk for a man, and it's easy for him to slide into passivity if he meets with ridicule.

When It Doesn't Go as Planned . . .

When your husband isn't leading how you'd like, that's when a strong woman gets busy. Learn to ask open-ended questions that promote deeper understanding. Let him know that you're praying for him and that you're in it with him—connected to him, not competing. Questions that start with "how," "what," and "why" encourage reflection and allow for more detailed responses.

Lloyd and I had different approaches when it came to teaching the children spiritual values. His was story-based, and he asked good questions and used his gift of intuition to engage the kids spiritually. I liked more concrete teaching, and it took me a while to learn to appreciate his style. When the kids were teens, Lloyd's ability to draw them out and chat openly about spiritual topics was especially helpful. If I had insisted that my way of shaping our kids' spirituality was the right way or the only way, Lloyd would have been tempted to be passive to avoid rocking the boat.

Wouldn't it feel freeing to broaden your perspective and enjoy seeing your spouse feel admired, appreciated, and accepted for who he is on the journey to who he's becoming?

When we entrust our lives to our heavenly Father, being the wife of an imperfect man gets a lot easier, particularly when we have disagreements. Lloyd and I make important decisions together, and that often takes time as we weigh each other's thoughts and concerns. With trust and commitment as foundational supports for our covenant marriage, I have found it easier to be willing to blend my perspectives, my preferences, and my thoughts with his, and learn to appreciate his point of view. This feels like the art, not just the science, of marriage. Only God can meet all my needs. My faith in God has grown as I've learned not to expect Lloyd to be the one who plays that role.

Today I'm more skilled at knowing when to speak up, when to shut up, and how to have those conversations with more care and finesse. This is hard, ongoing work, but it's good work. As you practice these skills, your children are learning valuable lessons, especially as you let them in on your journey of walking with God, going through rupture and repair cycles, and learning to do life Christianly. They'll be blessed to live in a home where mutual honor is prioritized.

In addition to submission for wives, all Christians are called to be meek. Being meek means we don't need to force our way in life. It goes hand in hand with the helpfulness of submission, like the icing on the cake. I like Elisabeth Elliot's description of meekness in her book *Keep a Quiet Heart*:

> Meekness is teachability. "The meek will he teach his way" (Ps. 25:9). It is the readiness to be shown, which includes the readiness to lay down my fixed notions, my objections and "what ifs" or "but what abouts," my certainties about the right-ness of what I have always done or thought or said. . . . Meekness is an explicitly spiritual quality, a fruit of the Spirit, learned, not inherited. It shows in the kind of attention we pay to one another, the tone of voice we use, the facial expression. . . . But how shall I, not born with the smallest shred of that quality, I who love victory by argument and put-down, ever learn that holy meekness? The prophet Zephaniah tells us to seek it (Zeph. 2:3). We must walk (live) in the Spirit, not gratifying the desires of the sinful nature (for example, my desire to answer back, to offer excuses and accusations, my desire to show up the other's fault instead of to be shown my own). We must "clothe" ourselves (Col. 3:12) with meekness—put it on, like a garment. This entails an explicit choice: I will be meek. I will not sulk, will not retaliate, will not carry a chip.[2]

2. Elisabeth Elliot, *Keep a Quiet Heart* (Grand Rapids: Revell, 2022 [1995 original]), 107–108.

As I wrestled with submission and meekness in my own life, I learned by trial and error. While I'm still a work in progress, I like what I've learned so far! As I seemingly gave up some of my "rights," I gained influence and skills that I had never thought of. God granted me patience as I stopped insisting on my timetable for working through disagreements. Choosing to focus on Lloyd's strengths instead of criticizing his weaknesses allows me to feel more content and grateful. When Lloyd knows I'm "for" him and believe in him, and we are building this covenant marriage together, he has a safe place to talk through anything and everything. When he can be open with me, my thoughts and opinions begin to carry greater weight.

Make It Yours

 READ Juli Slattery's book *Finding the Hero in Your Husband* is a wonderful book for framing a biblical view of a woman's power.

 TALK Make a few highlights in this chapter about paradoxes and read them with your spouse. What is his reaction? What makes him nervous about his role in the family? Ask him how you could be helpful.

 PLAN On your calendar, write down your husband's responses about how you could support his role in the family. Have them show up on your phone periodically as reminders.

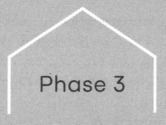

Phase 3

THE INTERIOR

A Wise Mom's Connection with Her Kids

Lots of work gets done inside a home. The pace of construction in a wise mom's home-building accelerates as a kitchen, bathrooms, electrical, and plumbing get installed. As children are born and "installed" in your family, you experience the exhilaration and hard work that goes into creating with care. The Bible acts as a blueprint of hope, comfort, and courage as you bend your back to the task of raising a family.

Phase Summary

Where would you be without a laundry room, a bathroom, or a kitchen? Our houses have spaces to keep us clean, healthy, and nourished, and in the same way, a wise mom building her home on Christ means she addresses topics that help her family function well on the inside.

In Chapter 9 you'll think about how you want to nourish your children's spiritual lives. Chapter 10 looks at incorporating healthy discipline in your children, a hot topic that always involves effort, learning, and prayer. We'll engage in conversations about sexuality from a Christian perspective in Chapter 11. This topic will give you plenty to talk about with family members, friends, and mentors.

Over time, you will begin to see the impact that the Bible's teaching is having in your family. The attitudes and behaviors you affirm are what you'll see more of. As you see healthy family patterns and habits beginning to grow in these internal areas, have fun celebrating the progress!

NURTURING YOUR CHILDREN'S SPIRITUAL GROWTH

I f I gave you a list of ten things you could do that would guarantee your child would grow up to love God and be a blessing in the world, would you do them?

The bad news is that there's no such list! But the good news is, while we don't get guarantees, we do get to influence our kids as we partner with God and model for them the great adventure of being a Jesus follower. Jesus said:

> These words I speak to you are not incidental additions to your life, homeowner improvements to your standard of living. They are foundational words, *words to build a life on*. If you work these words into your life, you are like a smart carpenter who built his house on solid rock. (Matt. 7:24–25)

Home is where we build our lives based on Jesus' teachings. The following verse reminds us of the value of having God's Word become part of the DNA of our family. It doesn't mean we have to have spiritual conversations all day long, but it suggests a variety of ways and times when those conversations can happen naturally. I'm grateful we can create families where having faith-based conversations is normative and doesn't only happen on Sundays.

Deuteronomy 6:6–7 advises us:

> Write these commandments that I've given you today on your hearts. Get them inside of you and then get them inside your children. Talk about them wherever you are, sitting at home or walking in the street; talk about them from the time you get up in the morning to when you fall into bed at night.

We have the privilege of introducing our children to our loving Creator.

> We have the privilege of introducing our children to our loving Creator.

Model and Train

Two of the tools we use to shape our children's spiritual lives are *model* and *train*:

1. We *model* an authentic spiritual life for our kids. More is caught than taught.
2. We *train* our children. We don't try to be a Christian family; we train to be one. Just like an athlete spends time practicing, there are things we can put into practice in our homes as well.

Like building the different parts of a house, nurturing happens over time, brick by brick: a bedtime or mealtime prayer habit, then Bible-verse memorizing and good Christian books and music. You might find the best time for teaching spiritual values is out in nature together, while your kids splash in the tub, at the kitchen table during a Bible-reading time together, or while riding in the car. My own kids, and now my grandkids, love Christian songs that are Bible verses set to music, which is a fun way to learn Scripture. When teaching young children to pray, in addition to scripted prayers, you can start with ordinary sentences: "I'm sorry. Please help me. Thank you." As your child gets older, they will build compassion and trust in God as you listen to their reports about what's happening in their friends' lives and pray about it with them.

There are so many ways to celebrate a relationship with God and enjoy the Bible together, so plan to form good habits in this area. For example, I remember a story of a boy who grew up in large Scottish family. Every morning after breakfast their dad, with his strong Scottish accent, would tell one of the children, "Get doon the Book." The Bible was kept on a shelf beside the table so it would be handy. Set yourself up for success, start small, and keep it sustainable.

What do modeling and training look like in your family so far? As you model for your kids, do they see you praying, reading the Bible, worshiping, confessing your faults, and making relational repairs?

If you're new to this aspect of building into your kids' lives, ask someone to walk alongside you to be a mentor and encourager. Perhaps friends from church who are a little further on their faith journeys can share what they enjoyed doing with their children and be a sounding board for you.

Memory Lane

Here are a few things that we practiced in our family: There was a big blackboard in the kitchen where we'd write a weekly Bible verse at the top, to discuss together. It seems small, but that adds up to fifty-two verses tucked away in young hearts and minds each year. Small, but mighty. Before the kids left for school, we'd read part of a Bible chapter; I still laugh thinking about how Lloyd would add funny comments or make a few changes to keep the kids' attention. I suggested we read a whole chapter each day, but Lloyd felt that we had many years to read together and it would be more sustainable to keep it short and sweet.

I loved reading to the kids and wanted them to become familiar with the Bible's stories. I greatly valued the privilege of doing that while they were preschoolers. Our children went to public school, so their curriculum wasn't specifically Bible-based. But at bedtime during their elementary years, I'd sit in the hall and read a combination of favorite books, Bible stories, and a devotional book. They usually fell asleep before we got through the pile!

When our son was in elementary school, I wanted him to read the first five books of the Bible. I knew there would be some tough sledding in there, so I offered to barter some favorite items he'd been wanting for time spent reading. Kids love an incentive, and let me tell you, his interest level went way up! I figured I couldn't expect the Holy Spirit to remind my kids of God's Word if I didn't deposit it in their hearts and minds in the first place.

Church was a weekly habit we built that became rewarding for us all. It was fun to attend baptism services as a family and hear the stories of people who were committing to being Jesus followers. As we became friends with and did Bible studies with other families, our kids enjoyed having Christian friends with similar values. We spent time eating together and being in each other's homes. Our kids got to see other ways of living out what it means to have a Christian marriage and family. When the kids were old enough, they helped with service projects and volunteered at church, in the community, and later with international serving opportunities.

Remember, we are all practicing. Not everything you try will be a good fit for your family. If something isn't working for you, your spouse, or your kids, you are free to pivot. Other families will model and train their children spiritually, and it will look different from what we did or what you may choose. This isn't about cramming your kids or your calendar with spiritual stuff or having look-alike families. It's about gently and intentionally weaving it into the fabric of daily life in a way that works for you.

Being a Christian family is not a passive endeavor. As we take specific actions with our little ones, God provides the long-term growth. Just as we enjoy seeing our children mature in the physical aspects of their lives, seeing them grow spiritually and develop their own relationships with God is a thrilling thing to experience.

This Is the Great Adventure

The excitement and adventure of being Jesus followers is communicated well in a song by Stephen Curtis Chapman called "The Great Adventure." The chorus says:

> Saddle up your horses; we've got a trail to blaze
>
> Through the wild blue yonder of God's amazing grace.
>
> Let's follow our leader into the glorious unknown.

This is the life like no other.

This is the Great Adventure.

The song captures the essence of some of the components of the Christian life that we want to share with the next generation.

My kids are now raising our grandkids. It's fun to see the in-town grandkids at church on Sunday. Their parents are making their own choices about their spiritual nurturing, and we now play a supporting role. I don't expect their experience to be identical to mine, but I'm encouraged to see them seeking wisdom from the Lord as they raise their little people.

Again, there isn't a set formula, but a family that loves each other, loves the Lord, and spends time in God's Word is going to instill strength from the inside out, strength that helps their home stand firm in the strongest storms, as Jesus describes in Matthew 7:24–25, which is worthy of quoting again with more detail:

> These words I speak to you are not incidental additions to your life, homeowner improvements to your standard of living. They are foundational words, words to build a life on. If you work these words into your life, you are like a smart carpenter who built his house on solid rock. Rain poured down, the river flooded, a tornado hit—but nothing moved that house. It was fixed to the rock.

Make It Yours

 READ *Faith Begins at Home* by Mark Holmen is a small, powerful book. You may have a more low-key style to your spiritual practices, but allow his thinking to spur your own as you think about a spiritual legacy for your children, grandchildren, and great-grandchildren. It certainly did for me!

 TALK Ask your husband if he has a preference for modeling or training when it comes to your children's spiritual growth. How can you encourage that? Does he have freedom to lead in a way that aligns with his personality and strengths?

 PLAN If you have family members who are Jesus followers, text and ask them to share resources they've found helpful. If not, a mentor or Jesus-following friends are good sources of information and encouragement as well.

10

DISCIPLINING YOUR CHILDREN

Sometimes I wonder whether disciplining with confidence is even possible in a culture with such an overwhelming array of options. From traditional to gentle, authoritative to permissive, parenting styles tend to swing back and forth like a pendulum!

The Bible has plenty to say about the discipline of children. It doesn't tell us exactly how that will look in each family, but it does give us some helpful guidelines. I'm inspired when I am with young parents and see how much they want the best for their children. I love watching how they creatively approach disciplining them, both the teaching and training, in ways that are Bible-based and suit their family's bents.

Discipline, like many of these topics, is best approached with a "learn as we go" attitude. If what you're doing is working for you and reflects what you see in the Bible, you are in an enviable place! If not, know that you can adapt your discipline style. You may even have to choose different styles for each of your children.

Your Early Years

Think back to how you were trained in your early years. If you're like me, you may have set ideas of things you do or don't want to pass on to your children. I was comfortable with how discipline was done in my family of origin, following traditional "spare the rod, spoil the child" thinking. Consequences beginning at a young age were one of the tools my parents used. Woven through their corrections were affirmations of love and value and their desire to see me learn obedience both to them and to God.

I saw that they cared enough about me to intervene using a variety of corrections and teaching/training styles geared to my particular needs. I learned that while I was deeply loved by God and my family, I was also a sinner in need of Jesus' forgiveness. Looking back, I am grateful for the boundaries that were put in place. I knew when I had crossed certain lines, and I understood what to expect when I did.

Fast-forward to my early parenting years: I was amazed at how soon my children understood when they were doing something wrong and how willing they were to test the boundaries we put in place! While I didn't enjoy the punitive side of disciplining them, I understood that I had a responsibility to make sure they learned how to acknowledge wrongdoing, repent, and be forgiven.

Lloyd and I chose to discipline them in a way that wiped the slate of wrongdoing clean; each child could experience forgiveness, total inclusion, and acceptance. It was a rupture and repair that strengthened, not diminished, our relationships with each child. I wanted my kids to learn to be humble and ask God for his help as they navigated living in a family and in the broader world outside our home. Our children grew to understand that our discipline wasn't something we did "to" them but was something we did "for" them.

Discipline Styles

Each child is unique. While some learn from a simple glance or redirection, others need clearer correction and consequences. It was interesting to see our son by age two learn that a gentle slap on the palm of his hand, along with a clear "no," meant he needed to change his habit of sliding his bowl of food off his high chair and on to the floor. At first I was afraid to do that; he seemed so young. It was eye-opening to see how quickly he changed his ways, resulting in more fun and less chaos for us all.

Lloyd and I weren't fans of grounding a child for misbehavior. It felt like punishment for us as we kept track of who was grounded for what. Instead, we worked to choose a punishment that fit the crime, that had meaning for the child. I remember when one of our kids was being disobedient on a long car trip, creating havoc for the rest of the family. They were warned that if they kept it up, they would have to stay in the car ten additional minutes once we arrived. They kept up the behavior, hoping we wouldn't make good on our statement. The result was the longest ten minutes of our lives as they waited until they could be released to play with their cousins. It was also the last time they chose to act like that on a car trip. "I hope you'll make a better choice next time" was something my kids heard when they had to suffer the consequences of their disobedience! When faced with consequences, our children are smart enough to make better choices in the future.

Your story and your way of training your children may look quite different than mine. Plenty of parents are wary of using punitive consequences based on their experiences. If you feel nervous or unsure of how physical discipline can be implemented well, read Chip Ingram's book *Effective Parenting in a Defective World*. In his chapter titled "Punishment Versus Discipline," he outlines seven important steps to consider. His balanced approach helped me feel more comfortable as I sought to modify my children's attitudes and behaviors, while wanting to be sure to maintain a loving bond between us. No matter what discipline style you choose, I'll be cheering you on as you invest in disciplining well! And remember, it's OK to explore multiple avenues of teaching and training your kids in a way that works for you.

The Gift of Discipline

We give our kids a gift when we teach and train them. Regardless of how the details play out in your particular family, imagine the potential results. Imagine that a child grows up in a family where there is a lot of love but also clear limits and consequences. The parents lean into learning about their child's emotions and brain development in the early years and distinguish between childishness and willfulness.

> We give our kids a gift when we teach and train them.

In our scenario, the parents recognize that sometimes it is in their child's best interest to enforce things that the child dislikes, such as sharing, self-control, or submitting to their mom and dad's authority. Along the way, the child learns how God created them in his image and loves them deeply. As they experience how sin has affected each of us and our need for forgiveness, they begin to establish their own relationship with God in a basic and sweet way. Early training, where external discipline is taught, grows to encapsulate the broader benefits of discipline, and they begin making their own internalized choices. Teenagers and young adults will have something solid to come back to, even if they seemingly walk away from some of their early training. Our goal is not to control but to sow good seed and trust God for a future harvest. So much of training and teaching around discipline is intertwined with nurturing our children spiritually.

While our imagined scenario can sound idealistic, we know that the rubber meets the road in the context of living as Christian human beings in a fallen world that the rubber meets the road. We realize very quickly how much we need God's help and wisdom as we raise and disciple these little people. I get a chuckle out of the phrase "raising children." I often felt that God was raising me as I experienced one parenting scenario after another that allowed me to see that I didn't have all the answers and needed his help.

Chaos vs. Peace

When a home is chaotic, with children and their emotions leading the charge, there is often a weariness and despair that sets in. Parenting children who have not yet been restrained from acting out of selfishness, defiance, and willfulness is an endurance test of unbelievable proportions. But children who are given the gift of discipline are often relieved; they feel assured that their parents care about them and mean what they say. Hebrews 12:11 encourages us to take the long view as we teach and train our young children: "At the time, discipline isn't much fun. It always feels like it's going against the grain. Later, of course, it pays off big-time, for it's the well-trained who find themselves mature in their relationship with God."

Talk with your spouse and agree to support each other even if you choose different discipline styles. Many families tend to have a parent who takes a firmer stance on discipline and one who is more of a "softie"; make sure your children don't play you against each other. Disagreements over how we handle discipline have the potential to create boatloads of conflict, and if exhaustion and chaos become a pattern, your home isn't going to be a welcoming place for anyone in the family, and you won't be able to bring your best. Spend time reading the book of Proverbs and pray for God's wisdom as you invest energy into this life-giving benefit for your children.

Make It Yours

 READ A book with good, common-sense guidelines is Ginger Hubbard's *Don't Make Me Count to Three!* Also, *The Whole-Brain Child* by Daniel J. Siegel and Tina Payne Bryson helps parents understand their children's brain development and learn to discern between childishness and willfulness.

 TALK As you and your spouse learn in this area, keep checking in with each other and ask God for hearts that are willing to grow and be open to each other's perspectives.

 PLAN On your phone, download a Bible-based podcast about training children that you can listen to as you go for a walk or run.

11

NAVIGATING SEXUAL-WHOLENESS TOPICS

How do you want your children to learn about sexuality topics? Would you prefer they learn from your worldview anchored in following Jesus or from other worldviews? What do you stand to gain by starting these conversations while your children are still young? Perhaps a more useful question to ask is what you stand to lose by *not* starting these conversations while your children are still young. If you delay speaking to your children about sexual topics, you may discover that they've already heard plenty from other sources, sometimes in unexpected and potentially harmful ways.

The Preparation

No amount of preparation will remove all the awkwardness of these conversations, but preparation certainly helps. The first step is to think back in time: What type of teaching or healthy framing around sexuality did you and your spouse get in your families of origin? This is another great date-night question to put in your phone! If you have things in your background that make sexuality conversations challenging, a Christian counselor or mentor can walk you through that gently. God's heart is for us, and you can trust him as you direct your energies to the future.

Second, think about what you saw modeled when you were growing up. In much of family life, more is caught than taught. You may have learned the art of expressing everyday personal affection with tenderness, eye contact, smiles, and expressions that you picked up along the way, or perhaps you did not see these little acts as often, or ever. Families where the husband and wife call each other "Honey," "Love," and "Dear" are affected positively by the love shown, and children thrive in an environment where they are addressed affectionately as well. This may be an area where you want to reach out for help with healing negative influences from your family of origin. This is important work, as is discussing with your spouse how you want to implement this topic in your own family.

As kids grow, their worlds grow as well. In the early years, your kids are largely protected from viewpoints that don't align with the Bible's teachings. Your instruction will be focused on God's wonderful creation of us as boys and girls, men and women. Those years of innocence don't last long. As your child gets older, it can be helpful to jot down a list of what makes up their world: friends, school, sleepovers, dances, movies, etc. What areas do you and your spouse see as concerns now or for the near future? Are there risky situations you want to avoid?

When our children were young, we had a few trusted families with whom they could have sleepovers. During their school-age years, when they watched a movie with friends in the neighborhood, our kids checked with us first. They knew to say, "Mom and Dad have a rule that we have to check in and let them know what movie we're watching." Since we didn't want to discuss more mature topics with them before they were ready, we set boundaries in place for their protection, both from exposure to culture-based sexuality and from images that we felt were too scary or violent. In older grades our kids occasionally attended school dances, but when we weren't comfortable with the dances, we arranged family trips instead. Each family gets to pray and then choose how they want to handle these sorts of things. I would never say anyone else should copy my choices. It's not that simple. I would encourage you to think, pray, and make a plan for your own family.

Perhaps you need to practice new ways of showing affectionate connection or practice setting boundaries around the places you don't want your kids to go. This may feel awkward at first; that's OK. You're not learning something new! Open, straightforward conversations with their parents will be a blessing to your kids as they hear the truth and learn that they can expect honest answers.

> *Your kids will hear the truth and learn to expect honest answers.*

Age-Appropriate Education

While your kids are young, teach them about privacy with their bodies and equip them to handle unwanted touches from other people. Have conversations in the home about what is and isn't allowed while playing doctor or when kids take a shared bath. Use age-appropriate books with your children as you begin the conversations.

We need to educate ourselves to have wise conversations with our kids. You can never start educating yourself too early. Even before they become teenagers, your kids will have plenty of questions about other people's sexual choices and orientations.

For Christian parents with children in public schools, sexual education curriculum is a challenging topic. We have his promised help and guidance as we think through school options for our children and respectfully express concerns in conversations with school administrators. Remember, the Bible encourages us to "be ready to speak up and tell anyone who asks why you're living the way you are, and always with the utmost courtesy" (1 Pet. 3:15).

Your Toolbox

Begin to build a simple toolbox of resources for educating your children. These can include books, articles, and videos, or even mentors and other parents. Part of the preparation is to learn what the Bible teaches about sexuality so that you are not just responding based on the opinions of others. God's commandments for us are just that—for us. We can stand firm in our convictions, knowing that what the Bible teaches about human sexuality reflects God's loving heart to provide us with his best, not to limit our freedom. The limits God sets for us sexually are for our good and protection. A wood fire in a fireplace is a wonderful thing—the heat, the crackling logs, the woodsmoke—but a fire that escapes the fireplace can burn down a house. That perspective is important for your children to understand as they grow. Are you willing to have strong convictions and calmly, lovingly live by them?

We want our children to bring their questions to us, no matter how uncomfortable or surprising they may be. My friend Traci Lester speaks at MomsMentoring gatherings and gives us a world-class response for when our kids ask us disconcerting questions. Her recommended response to our kids is, "I'm so glad you asked." Thinking the topics through ahead of time and being prepared allows this ongoing discussion to happen in a more matter-of-fact way, like brushing your teeth.

My friend Jenna shared that the many conversations she and her husband have had with their girls over the years have removed most of the awkwardness. Your kids will be exposed to sexual ideas and content much earlier than you likely anticipate. By starting early you ensure that when your kids hear untruths about sexuality later, they already know the truth. What a privilege to talk with your kids about sexuality, without fear and in the privacy of your own home, teaching them about this life-giving gift God has provided for us.

Make It Yours

 READ Traci Lester's book *Teaching the Birds and the Bees Without the Butterflies* is a practical guide, and *How and When to Tell Your Kids About Sex* by Stan and Brenna Jones is the parents' guide in the excellent God's Design for Sex series.

 TALK Understanding where you and your husband are coming from is helpful as you discuss how you want to handle this topic in your own family. I like the subtitle of the Joneses' book mentioned above: *A Lifelong Approach to Shaping Your Child's Sexual Character.* Like spiritual conversations, these conversations happen little by little.

 PLAN Make a recurring note in your calendar to revisit this topic every year, as you and your spouse decide next steps as your children grow.

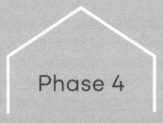

Phase 4

THE WINDOWS
AND DOORS

*A Family's Connection with the
World Beyond Their Home*

Your family is being formed. You are having fun with a kaleidoscope of activities, growth, and learning, and many of these things happen inside your home in the early years. You feel elated as your children grow and hit milestones. Eventually, many of their experiences will happen away from home. Like windows and doors that let you see and access the world outside, your teachings and perspectives will shape your kids' views and interactions with their broader culture, long after they launch from home.

Phase Summary

There are big changes happening in our culture and our world, which means we'll have to be prayerful and thoughtful as we engage in interactions with our culture. As you make decisions about the ins and outs of your family's interactions in the broader world, you'll want to shape your children's worldview based on the Bible's teachings and a "love God, love others" mentality.

In Chapter 12 we'll explore how creating family values and a family vision gives you tracks to follow as you decide the yeses and noes of life. Chapter 13 is fun! You'll see how your position as a CLO—a Chief Life Officer—will inspire you to learn and make choices that align with who God has made you to be, giving you the confidence to build a one-of-a-kind family. Technology in the family takes center stage in Chapter 14, and Chapter 15 is a final look at engaging well with our culture.

12

CREATING A FAMILY VISION BASED ON YOUR VALUES

Sitting around a bonfire with our kids when they were nine, seven, and five years old, we asked them to weigh in on "what's working in our family" and "what's not working in our family." Their responses were so enlightening! After listening to them share from their hearts, we told them that we could all decide the kind of family we wanted to be. We could write it out and help each other grow into that family.

Now, more than thirty years later, that small investment of time and intentionality has shaped who our family has become. We never would have guessed how much can grow from a small amount of intentionality.

To determine what kind of family we wanted to be, we wrote six family values on a sheet of paper. These values gave us tracks to follow and helped us decide our yeses and noes as life brought opportunities and challenges. That sheet of paper lived on our fridge for the next fifteen years, and it became more valuable as the kids got older.

Reeb Family Values, 2002

As a family we value the following six things, and we plan to invest in activities that support these values:

- *Jesus Followers*—Above all else we want our family to reflect God's love and character in our world.
- *Love in Action*—We will spend time with each other, serving each other, being generous with each other, and serving those in need right around us in our community.
- *Together Memories*—We will plan both fun adventures and unstructured goofing-off time together.
- *Celebrating Individual Interests*—We will know what each family member is passionate about and support their interest in those areas.
- *Unique Individuals*—We will take the time to know and understand each other's unique personalities, strengths, and dreams so that we can help each other flourish.
- *Enthusiasm*—We will bring a positive, constructive attitude.

As our children grew, we would look at the list and ask ourselves how we were doing.

Sticking to these guidelines can seem a bit rigid, but it gave us a lot of freedom. For instance, because one of our values was creating "Together Memories," we found the confidence and rationale to eliminate some of the busyness our culture imposes on young families. We decided to set a limit on extracurricular activities because we agreed that it was trading up, not giving up, to focus on having consistent, memory-making family times with deep connection.

Another family value of ours is to understand each other well and get behind our individual interests. As the kids got older, we learned each other's love languages, took personality assessments like Myers-Briggs, and identified each person's top strengths. This helped us understand each family member and leveled the playing field as we learned each other's strengths and struggles. The kids felt affirmed by seeing their whole family keenly interested in them and applauding their uniqueness. Over time they began to see who God designed each family member to be, learned what made them tick, and appreciated the God-given strengths and gifts they'd been given. It felt like a puzzle coming together and helped play down sibling rivalry.

When the kids were older, we boiled our values down into a vision statement, which read like this:

Intentional Jesus followers who support and know each other well.

Enjoying eating, playing, encouraging each other, and traveling together.

Sharing God's love in our own unique ways with the communities around us.

Then and Now

This vision has become a part of our children's lives and affects their interactions as adults in their thirties. For example, our daughter-in-law, Shanna, is the only person in our extended family with the strength of command. We rely on her thoughtful, kind ability to make decisions and give direction when things get complicated. She does this naturally both in the family and with her nonprofit work, where she serves seniors. The top strength of her husband—our son, Carter—is empathy; we all benefit from that, as he is quick to understand when anyone needs a little extra TLC. Our son-in-law Jochen and daughter Caroline work with a student ministry in Germany, and it's fun to see their interest in reaching out to the students, sharing the good news of the gospel, and living with the people they serve and feed. Our youngest daughter, Jennie, and her husband, Chris, have a heart for community and invest in the lives of their young family and the neighbors and colleagues they rub elbows with every day. We have some family members who love to cook and others who are practical jokers and game players. We still enjoy traveling together, and watching the grandkids interact has become a fun pastime for us all.

Like any family with lots of personalities, we will always have to do the work of extending grace, forgiving and being forgiven, overlooking offenses, and having crucial conversations that build the family up. A quality family never just happens, and we are often reminded that we need God's help to intentionally live out our family vision. Thankfully, there is no aspect of family life that God doesn't care about. As 1 Peter 5:7 reminds us, "Live carefree before God; he is most careful with you."

Years ago, our friends Jerel and Susan Law came up with a different list of values for their much younger family.

Law Family Laws

1. Everybody helps everybody.
2. Be positive and encouraging.
3. The kids are to listen and obey the parents—always!
4. Respect one another's space and stuff.
5. Help each other make wise choices.

6. Remember, "please" and "thank you" are the signs of a grateful heart.
7. Be quick to rally around a family member who is down.
8. Eat as many meals together as possible.
9. Have a lot of FUN!
10. God is number one in our family.

At first they had a typo, and number eight said, "Eat as many meals as possible." That made for a few laughs!

Families can have a blast with this exercise as they create their own set of values. Maybe your family will even decide to revise it every year—there are no rules for this exercise, so have fun with it!

Without a clear vision, many families drift along with the culture. A family vision can help you stay focused on your shared values. Ours gave us stability when everything was going well and when we hit the inevitable rough patches that came to each of us. Life seemed more fun, and less risky, when we were intentionally aligned with God's priorities, using what he had blessed us with. We wanted to learn to love and care for each other and those around us, and we created space in our family life to do that. You can't be every kind of family, so why not take stock of who you are and what you value, and then partner with God based on that?

> A family vision can help you stay focused on your shared values.

Make It Yours

 READ *Habits of the Household* by Justin Whitmel Earley gives an inspirational look at family habits and how those habits shape family culture.

 TALK Consider with your spouse any spoken or unspoken values that have shaped your family culture so far. Are there any you would like to delete, amend, or add?

 PLAN What's fun for you and your kids? It could be a special meal, bonfire, or hike. During the activity, create a note together, listing your family values. If your children are old enough to weigh in, include their ideas too. Whittle them down to five or so, then print them out and put them where you can see them often. Set a recurring reminder on your phone to chat about how it's going with your family values.

13

BEING A
CHIEF LIFE OFFICER

We might not be a CEO or COO in the corporate world, but as moms we are all in the C-suites of our families as CLOs—Chief Life Officers, partnering with God to build our one-and-only lives alongside him. God can use each one of us if we just partner with him, listening and turning ideas into action.

My Story

In my thirties I enjoyed a variety of activities. I worked in a dental office part-time, taught Sunday school, was a room mom at school, and volunteered at Habitat for Humanity. I also hosted a life group, led a book club in my neighborhood, and played in the band at church. We enjoyed inviting people over for meals and hosting overnight guests. It was all quite fun until I experienced a year of panic attacks and another year of recovery. Then I had some CLO choices to make. I couldn't do fifteen different things anymore. If I wanted to function well, I could only manage a couple of activities.

Who was I going to be?

During that time, as I mentioned before, I took a personality assessment and learned my strengths and spiritual gifts.

God worked in my heart to teach me some needed humility and empathy. Feeling weak was a new experience. The impact of our friends' divorces and God's nudge to move in the direction of encouraging other moms started to take root. I started to sink myself deeply into who God had made me to be, and I began saying no to what was not mine to do. My new mantra, when I was asked to do things that didn't align with my emerging mission, was "Thanks for asking. I wish I could, but I can't." I hope I never go through that painful trial again, but the learning that came from it was invaluable.

Over the years, Lloyd and I have had to ask ourselves whether we are willing to make choices as Jesus-centered CLOs or go on autopilot and default to a combination of the culture around us and how we were raised. It's a tough question! A thriving family, built on Christ, requires planning, skills, and intentionality. Thankfully, a thriving family is not a perfect family, because there is no such thing! Our job is to manage decisions so that our family families thrive in ways that make our homes a place we want to be. Let's play out some hypothetical scenarios to get a feeling for some of the choices that go into building a thriving family.

> Our job is to manage decisions so that our family thrives.

Family 1 vs. Family 2

Family 1 liked to relax and drift along—life was good for them. They reacted to what came at them and tried to fit it all into their calendar. While they had a spiritual component to their lives, other activities sometimes managed to squeeze out their good intentions of regular church attendance and time to nurture their personal relationship with the Lord. Worthwhile causes, fun activities, and vacations based on cultural expectations kept things lively. Sometimes they felt a little breathless at the pace of life and a little scattered as they reacted to all the things that came across their path.

Family 2 decided that a little intentionality might serve them well. They planned their calendars so that high-value items got prioritized and repeated while a "smiling no" was given for lesser-value items. They chose serving opportunities and recreation that aligned with their commitment to healthy life habits and caring relationships. Church attendance, along with time for spiritual growth and training, was a regular part of their lives.

Read back through the two families. What strikes you? In some ways Family 1 might seem to have an easier life, more laidback and unstructured. But I imagine that they are sometimes tired and overwhelmed with the busyness of life. Will they look back in twenty years and say that they exchanged priceless things for merely valuable things?

Family 2 exerts more effort to decide priorities and values on the front end. I'm guessing that since they choose activities that align with their values and say no to things that don't, their hindsight after twenty years will generate gratitude for the priceless things that got embedded into their family. In giving a "smiling no," they may experience less exhaustion and be better able to focus on the things that matter to them. This is the essence of a well-curated life.

Thinking Ahead

Lloyd and I have facilitated couples' weekends for years as part of his ministry at the Halftime Institute. I have spent lots of time with many families who resemble both Family 1 and Family 2. Now their children have grown, and while there's no single pattern that emerges for everyone, I hear many Family 1 parents share that they wish they had been more intentional about their spiritual lives, prioritized their marriages, and operated based on their own values instead of on their peer groups or the culture around them.

This helped me think ahead to what I wanted for my own family. Here are some helpful questions to get you started:

- What are priorities in your family? Would it serve you well to identify things in your calendar that you can put on repeat and avoid making ongoing decisions about?
- How do your kids' social and sports activities best fit into the family? Are there any healthy limits that need to be set at this season?
- What will Sabbath rest and downtime look like for your family?
- What will a "smiling no" look like when you're asked to participate in things that don't align with the values you have as a family?

Intentional Choices

One mom I know wrote a letter to her parents and in-laws explaining why she and her husband don't want them to buy more than one gift for each grandchild at Christmas. She suggested giving activities and events together as an alternative.

Another mom opted out of spending an important holiday with a branch of the family that had radically different lifestyles and perspectives on gender and sexuality. She explained to the family that, while they were dearly loved, she and her husband had children at an age where having conversations about the situation was not advisable. They showed love and respect to the extended family members, but they also drew a boundary for what did not work for their immediate family in that season. Making intentional, loving choices instead of feeling burdened by expectations and obligations can be a refreshing way to do life!

Read Galatians 6:4–5 and reflect on what you will cultivate to become more of a Chief Life Officer in your own life:

> Make a careful exploration of who you are and the work you have been given, and then sink yourself into that. Don't be impressed with yourself. Don't compare yourself with others. Each of you must take responsibility for doing the creative best you can with your own life.

This is truly one of my favorite mom verses—and topics! As I developed more clarity about what I wanted for my own life, even when it looked different from others, I learned to compete less and compare less. I was able to celebrate the diversity of many different types of good families. I felt freed as I watched judgment, competition, and comparison go down the drain. Doing the "creative best" I can with my own life—I could get used to that kind of freedom!

Make It Yours

 READ Our friends Bill and Carolyn Wellons combined intentionality and fun by taking a yearly trip to think through their lives together and plan for the future. Read the workbook they created based on their experiences, *Getting Away to Get It Together*.

 TALK Ask some friends you admire and who have older kids how they learned to make decisions about their life choices.

 PLAN Use your phone to make a list of all the components of your life. Assign a rating from one through five for each of them based on your values and personality. Can you omit any of them or rework them to align with your preferences and preferred pace of life?

14

PROTECTING YOUR FAMILY FROM THE DOWNSIDE OF TECHNOLOGY

There's no denying that we live in a tech-saturated world. Technology is a learning tool, an ever-changing communication vehicle, and a vital part of real social connection, and yet we want to protect our families from aspects that can be harmful. What do we need to safeguard our families but stay current and engaged in our culture?

While we can't predict where technology will take us, we can get clear on the desired results from our engagement with it. We can write out our goals so that we have the courage and grit to stick with those goals and protect the boundaries we ultimately set.

Only you can decide what your desired results are—each family is different. I encourage you to make a list, and then as your children get older, let your desired results be a topic of conversation before they become a tug of war. If you teach children in their early elementary years that, when they eventually get a phone, there will be limits on screen time in the evenings, tech won't be used during family meals, and there will be scheduled unplugged time, it becomes expected long before it's actually happening. Paint a word picture of the fun you will have as a family in coming years, with screens and technology playing a part in the mix along with traveling, sports, friendships, and other activities.

Two Practices

As we consider this topic, let's look at it from two perspectives. One perspective is preparing the child for the path, and the other is preparing the path for the child. Think about these two perspectives as you plan; your family technology plan may combine elements of both.

Preparing the child for the path includes talking about technology use, getting your children's input, discussing media consumption from a Christian perspective, and helping each other keep on track. Your kids will develop a strong ethics base as you work through this together over many years. If they are exposed to Bible-influenced discussions, they will come to see that God's commandments for them are just that—*for* them, for their good!

> God's commandments for them are just that—for them, for their good!

Romans 12, which is full of wisdom for family life, has some helpful guidelines to discuss with your children:

- "Don't become so well-adjusted to your culture that you fit into it without even thinking" (Rom. 12:2).
- "Run for dear life from evil; hold on for dear life to good" (Rom. 12:9).

I remember when one of our kids announced that, because they were turning thirteen, they could now watch PG-13 movies. At the time, I was forty-two, and we had an interesting conversation about how, at my age, I could watch anything I wanted. We talked about how being a Jesus-follower weighed in on my choices. Through that conversation I guided her to think through the fact that just because you *can* do something, that doesn't mean you *should* do something.

Think deeply about the time your family spends on entertainment and technology. Is there any downside to the amount of time and money you spend in those two areas? Discuss this with your spouse and make a note in your phone to revisit this question each year.

I remember chatting with a friend who was surprised that I hadn't seen a specific movie as a child. He commented that it probably was because my family had all girls. I know for a fact that if I'd had brothers, they wouldn't have watched that movie either. My parents had predecided that violent movies showing people getting killed were not something they were comfortable showing to children, whether girls or boys.

Again, every family chooses for themselves. But as families of faith, let's make sure we think long and hard about the choices we make and partner with God in the process. Kids may not always appreciate the choices parents make in their formative years, but if limits are set in a fair and loving way and are combined with open communication, the kids will come to see that the parents had their best interests at heart.

Preparing the path for the child involves what sources of technology you have in your home, in what quantity, and in what rooms. As Christian families we need to be honest with ourselves. Is having TVs, screens, and phones in our bedrooms going to be the best for our families? When I had three young children, I thoroughly enjoyed the reprieve I got when my little ones could watch an educational show while I prepared dinner. I was also grateful that we decided not to watch television during the rest of the day. It was an occasional activity in our home, which left lots of time in the preschool years for reading, crafts, playing, chores, outdoor fun, and music.

Now, when I babysit my grandchildren, I'm reminded of the effort that must be expended to direct how time gets spent. When my grandkids beg for one more episode of their favorite show, it can be tempting to give in to what's easy and convenient if I haven't mentally prepared for what's next. There are a few groans when the TV gets shut off, but the show fades into the background as we head to the playground or have fun making granola together.

Philippians 4:8 provides a helpful framework for our analysis of technology use:

> Summing it all up, friends, I'd say you'll do best by
> filling your minds and meditating on things true, noble,
> reputable, authentic, compelling, gracious—the best, not
> the worst; the beautiful, not the ugly; things to praise,
> not things to curse.

Imagine reading the following verse with your children as they grow up and leave your home: "Put into practice what you learned from me, what you heard and saw and realized" (Phil. 4:9). What things will your children have learned, received, heard, and seen in you that will benefit them in their young adult lives?

Questions to Start With

Here are some big-picture questions on this ever-changing topic:

- Are you and your spouse happy with the media and internet you consume as adults? How do you determine what you will or won't watch or listen to and the amount of time you spend?
- Do you feel anxious about helping your kids balance technology choices? What research do you need to do around the effects of technology, video games, and social media?
- As your children grow, how will you assess when your kids are being harmed from too much exposure to technology or social media? How will you know if they are exposed to damaging content? How will you and your spouse become a comfortable and safe place for your children to discuss what they see or hear and what is going on with their friends?
- What other Christian families do you know who have walked this path in a way you respect? Could you ask for their recommendations?

Make It Yours

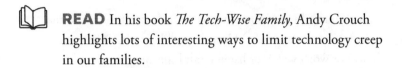 **READ** In his book *The Tech-Wise Family*, Andy Crouch highlights lots of interesting ways to limit technology creep in our families.

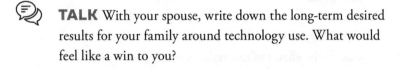 **TALK** With your spouse, write down the long-term desired results for your family around technology use. What would feel like a win to you?

PLAN Use your phone to set a yearly reminder to review and revise your tech plan together as a couple.

15

INTERACTING AS A FAMILY OF FAITH IN TODAY'S WORLD

The windows and doors in our homes both protect and give access to the world outside our four walls. Living out our faith in Jesus can feel like the finishing touches that go into making a house a home. Your family will decide if you prefer screen doors or storm doors; window shades or curtains; a bonfire pit or a vegetable garden—all the things that make your home yours.

Here are some components of a Christian home. As you read through them, think about what they could look like in your life.

Faith in God's Promises

Is God good? Can I trust him? When your children leave home someday, they might not know for sure what their own answer would be to these two questions, but they will know what you and your spouse believe.

Will they have witnessed their mom and dad's deep belief in the goodness of God? Will they have seen faith front and center, both in their home and in the way their family interacted with others? As they witnessed happy and sad times, peaceful and stressful family events of every sort over the years, will they have seen you walking with God through it all—the good, the bad, and the ugly? Will they know that a salvation life is about a living relationship, not just a collection of ideas?

Faith often feels a little private, and it can take practice to live it out loud, even in front of your children. My friend Amy likes to dance as she sings praise songs during her devotional time, and she includes her preschoolers. Another mom "greets the day" with her daughter. Wrapped in warm blankets on the back porch, they pause before leaving for school to speak to God, thanking him and praising his creativity as they enjoy the sunrise sky together. Short but sweet.

A Lifestyle That Promotes Well-Being

With dependence on God, you get to make choices and decisions that align with the Bible's teachings yet are based on your personality and bent. This will ensure that you won't be a cookie-cutter family but will be one of a kind!

Everything from sacred to secular can fit in this category, including nutrition, exercise, regular prayer and Bible reading, practicing servant-hearted interactions, being hospitable, showing compassion, caring for people's needs in your relationship circles, making quality entertainment choices, and becoming kind-spoken. Will the neighbors up and down the street see anything different about your family that reflects Christlikeness? Chat with your spouse about these categories and others that are important to you. Are you happy with the habits you've developed in these areas? What might you need to stop doing or start doing?

A Long View

Being a Christian family means keeping a long-term view in mind. It's tempting to take matters into your own hands and become a helicopter parent when you have concerns about your kids. While it's important to think through the influences and choices that affect your children, your best posture will be on your knees in prayer. The process of raising a family requires patience, like waiting for a garden to bloom.

I have a friend I call when I'm discouraged, and she takes a moment to pray right then and there—such an encouragement! You may be tempted to beat yourself up at times and think that you're not doing a good job. God can weave even failures and faults into a beautiful tapestry over time. He is happy to help, so trust him and focus on what is working as you go day by day.

> Raising a family requires patience, like waiting for a garden to bloom.

A Servant Heart

Being a Christian family challenges us to live unselfishly. Our homes are where we practice. What's the point of being kind to others if we can't be kind to each other? Galatians 5:22–23 describes some of the qualities God builds into our lives that will bless the people who live inside our homes as well as those in the broader community:

> But what happens when we live God's way? He brings gifts into our lives, much the same way that fruit appears in an orchard—things like affection for others, exuberance about life, serenity. We develop a willingness

> to stick with things, a sense of compassion in the
> heart, and a conviction that a basic holiness permeates
> things and people. We find ourselves involved in loyal
> commitments, not needing to force our way in life, able
> to marshal and direct our energies wisely.

I'm sensing in these verses a slow creation of daily lives that are open to being influenced by the Holy Spirit's presence and guidance. Pick something from these verses that looks like the type of fruit you'd love to see growing in your family. A quick online search will generate Bible verses that align. Print several out and discuss them so your family can cultivate that "fruit of the Spirit" together.

A Sense of Fun and Optimism

Joy, laughter, singing, and fun are gifts from God. Proverbs says, "A cheerful heart fills the day with song" (Prov. 15:15), and, "A merry heart does good, like medicine" (Prov. 17:22, NKJV). Faith and fun are not mutually exclusive! Christians, of all people, have reasons to be joyful—not in our circumstances perhaps, but deeper than that. Family life provides so many humorous moments, and our kids are often entertaining and hilarious. When you think of words like jolly, joyous, lively, laid-back, playful, and upbeat, do any of those words describe your family? Discuss as a family or with your spouse how you'd like to see more of that play out in your everyday lives.

Facing the Future Without Fear

Part of being a joy-filled family involves not letting fear have the upper hand in our lives. Last year we had a conversation with our extended family about our culture and the challenges of raising kids in today's world. Our daughter Jennie, who had an eight-month-old at the time, spoke up and gave a two-minute talk that I wish I could have recorded. I think every faith-based parent would have been encouraged to hear her articulate how she was not going to cave in to a fearful mindset for her children. She expressed confidence that God is in charge of what happens on planet Earth and is the same now as he has always been. Even though she doesn't know everything that will happen as she and her husband, Chris, raise their family, she affirmed their intentions to build their home on something they've found to be rock-solid.

As Jennie spoke these words, I could see her resolve to trust God; partner with him; and live assured of his love, care, and provision for her family, no matter what cultural storms may blow. She teared up a bit because of the force of her convictions, and my heart was encouraged to align with those convictions as well, to be an encourager and supporter of moms and dads worldwide as they raise the next generation.

Discuss with your spouse the areas where you each tend to act from a fearful perspective instead of a faith-filled perspective. How can you cheer each other on in these areas?

Real-Life Families

Here are some of my friends' stories about how it looked for their families to live out a Christian faith in today's world. Which of these stories resonates with you?

Vanessa prayed each summer for God's guidance about school choices for her girls—private, Christian, public, or homeschool? Each year she made up her mind to be open to whatever route God impressed on her and her husband. Remember, God will not get tired of your annual prayers!

Tara and George were wired by God to have their home be a neighborhood hub. Kids were always welcome. They spent a fortune on pizza, but they valued knowing their kids' friends and being able to share God's love with them. Their children developed a hospitality habit because of their example.

Beth's kids went through a public charter school. She incorporated a daily devotional into their rides to school and enjoyed having time to talk about it with them. Little by little, her children learned the value of seeing their daily lives intersected with the Bible's teachings.

Terry's family lived far away from their church, and it was tempting to opt out of the middle school youth group. Instead, she found a buddy nearby she could carpool with. She made sure her family regularly plugged into church and ensured her kids had opportunities to grow their faith alongside other kids.

Jen has her four boys' sports schedules and school calendars up on a huge sheet of glass in the kitchen. Right up there beside them are their family values, their Bible verse of the week, and their chores.

If you're new to this, take baby steps. Pray and ask God to provide a mentor or some like-minded friends who can offer support and encouragement, because this involves thought and effort. If you're a family that decides attending church weekly is part of who you are, you have one less decision to make every single week. You may be the type to allocate set times when the TV is on and off. Or not . . . but it may be important to you to discuss movies and music with your children from a spiritual perspective. As you can see, this involves intentionality, but it's worth it!

Romans 12:2 reminds us that drifting along with our culture isn't in our best interests: "Don't become so well-adjusted to your culture that you fit into it without even thinking. Instead, fix your attention on God. You'll be changed from the inside out."

You've got this! We're not aiming for perfect, but for intentional.

Make It Yours

 READ *The Shaping of a Christian Family* by Elisabeth Elliot isn't meant to be a "how-to" book. It is, however, an interesting peek into the lives of one Christian family around the turn of the previous century. As trends and themes and cultures come and go, it can be helpful to step back from the here and now and consider how people from an earlier era established their family culture.

 TALK Ask people you respect who have older children what being a Jesus-follower looks like in their family.

 PLAN Use your phone to download encouraging faith-based books you can listen to when you're on the go. You can have a virtual book club with your spouse, a friend, or a whole group. For young kids, catchy Bible verses set to music or a good faith-based story can make a car ride fun.

FINDING DEEP CONFIDENCE IN GOD AS YOU BUILD

How have you felt God's peace and encouragement as you think about the family you are building? God knows exactly what your children will face in their lifetimes—and he is not worried. Your kids are his first, and yours second.

While you will face many situations that tempt you to fret and worry, remember that you can partner with the God of the universe who loves your family and have him weigh in on each day as you build your home on Christ. God's plan is for our wholeness and health and joy. That's hard to beat!

The Bible is a well-rounded guide for family life at every level, but the Bible's ideas for how to live flow against the general direction of our culture today. Creating a safe place to question, search, and believe as you discuss these topics sets your kids up for having their own crucial conversations with peers as they get older, while modeling love instead of judgment.

Keep praying, and entrust yourself and your family to the One who says he will never leave or forsake us. We can boldly say, "The Lord is my helper; I will not fear" (Heb. 13:6, NKJV).

My prayer is that this book encourages you in your journey of becoming a wise mom, as you build your home on Christ.

ABOUT THE AUTHOR

LINDA RUTH REEB is the founder of MomsMentoring. Her passion is mentoring young mothers and helping them apply the Bible's wisdom to their lives. Linda has cowritten a book called *Halftime for Couples* with her husband, Lloyd, with whom she facilitates couples' events through the Halftime Institute. She enjoys spending time with her husband and keeping up with their three children and four grandchildren.